50
YEARS A VETERINARIAN

STORIES OF ANIMALS AND THEIR PEOPLE

Donald V. "Doc" Tebbe, D.V.M.

ISBN: 978-1-4834-6514-2 (sc)
ISBN: 978-1-4834-6513-5 (e)

Library of Congress Control Number: 2017901622

Lulu Publishing Services rev. date: 2/23/2017

FOREWORD

I never really believed in destiny or that things happen the way they are supposed to until May of 1993. I had a sweet, beautiful golden retriever named Molly. She would go to my flower shop with me every day. People loved her, not just my customers, but people in the community that no longer had pets came to see her in the flower shop. They would bring their relatives from out of town to meet her.

One warm May day while walking to the end of the shopping center there was a space with a big sign on the door, Veterinarian Coming Soon. "Molly, look you are going to have your very own Veterinarian to take care of you," I told her.

Time went by, and the vet moved in. We made and sold homemade fudge in the flower shop; it was even named after Molly, (Molly McFudge.) Well, it seems the Doc had a taste for all things sweet and fudge was one of his favorites. He would sneak down to the flower shop almost every day after lunch to get a little fudge.

His wife was in hospice and Doc would pick her up some fresh flowers every couple days. One day Molly was having trouble keeping her food down, so off we went to see Doc.

He knew she was sick and tried to break it to me gently. After a while of him poking and prodding her, taking her blood, and trying to boost her with cortisone Molly began to hate going down to see her loving vet. Doc started coming to see her at the flower shop so that she would not be scared.

We began trading services, he would treat my precious Molly, and I would make him lovely flowers to take to his wife. Sadly in the fall, my part of the barter turned to sadness making the flowers for Doc's wife's funeral. His wife had been sick for a couple of years, and Doc stood by her and loved her the best he could. He had been a good husband to her for 33 years.

A big chunk of my heart left me the day that Molly passed. Doc was sad too. My best friend was gone; the loving spirit that had not left my side for nine years, she had been with me day and night. She played in the ocean with me, and let me hold her when things got tough.

Doc had been through deep sadness living through the tough illness with his wife. One day, borrowing my daughter's brand new lifted Jeep I went to the vet clinic and told Doc, "Let's go, we could both use a beer." He was shy and unassuming, kind, and quiet. We sat in the bar for a while swapping stories about animals. I caught him staring at me; I asked," What are you looking at," He said, "I can't believe I am out with a young chicky like you." Oh, Geez, I thought.

The next day at the flower shop my best friends who worked with me asked, "Are you going out with Doc again?" I told them, "Are you kidding? I am not going out with someone that calls me a young chicky."

The girls got after me because they really liked Doc, he was steady, smart, a good salt of the earth kind of guy. They begged me to give him another chance, especially since all the other men in my life had turned out to be schmucks. Doc was a little old fashioned but certainly not a schmuck.

Molly gave me one final beautiful gift, the love of one of the kindest, loving people on earth. I have spent 22 beautiful years with my best friend watching him love and care for animals. This is my story of how I met my Doc, this book is his story, and I hope you enjoy reading them as much as he loves telling them.

Margie

PREFACE

Veterinarians as a group are good storytellers. Years of never knowing what the next animal brings in terms of danger, excitement, sorrow and satisfaction that builds a keen bond quickly between the vet, the animal and its' human. The emotions are often raw and dynamic. The real person at his or her best, and sometimes at their worst always shows up. When the dust settles and the old dog or injured gelding is taken care of, the vet asks, "What the hell was that all about?" It was all about a memory that becomes a story. Veterinarians have their heads full of stories that ought to be told.

The advice James Herriot gave to a young veterinarian wanting to write was, "Don't take yourself too seriously when you write. The stories are the play and your readers are the audience. Just enjoy the show and write about that." His story is tucked in one of 50 Years a Veterinarian chapters.

The stories in 50 Years a Veterinarian are all based on actual facts, however they are written in "slant", meaning with some degree of embellishment, but not much. Ride with a vet on a Sunday morning call to a bloated cow, the delivery of a satanic freak calf or come face to face with a real ghost This vet is no hero, but he is interesting.

"Doc"

This book is dedicated to all the animals who have given me such an incredible life, and to my beautiful family who never faltered in their love for me.

CONTENTS

Monday, June 18, 1962

Joy, enthusiasm in hyper drive, confidence, and anticipation all bubbling over at the same time, described the feeling of this brand new veterinarian and his wife as we came into the town of Fort Recovery, Ohio, our new home. Ten days earlier, graduating from The Ohio State College of Veterinary Medicine allowed me the great privilege to be addressed as Doctor Tebbe, so I was pretty full of myself. Today was the day that prideful thinking would all come to an end. It sure didn't last long.

Mid-June in the farm countryside of Ohio was beautiful and warm. The earth smelled of things growing and newly cut alfalfa hay. Fort Recovery was going to be a perfect fit for us.

The first surprise greeted us as we drove into the driveway. Dr. Mitchner packed his family of seven into a sparkling new Buick. He wore a sharp-looking sports shirt and expensive slacks. The car was running.

Dr. Mitchner thought this was a good time to inform us that he was going on a month-long vacation with his family. It took him three minutes to introduce us to Gretta, the receptionist who collected all the money from the clients. She also knew where to find everything.

The smile on Dr. Mitchner's face showed the joy, the enthusiasm, and maybe, the confidence I had relished just a few short minutes ago.

He stepped into his car and said, "You'll be OK." Just like that, they left. Oh my gosh! I was as scared as a kid on his first date!

Zandy, the new Mrs. Tebbe, left to unpack the few things we owned and then she had an appointment to meet the school superintendent for her job interview at the grade school. The fourth-grade position was open.

played a big role in the decision to proceed with the anesthesia agent on hand. It certainly was not common sense. I soaked a few cotton balls with ether and slipped them into the box to subdue the little beast. It seemed like a good idea.

Pretty soon, the struggling noise died down, and opening the lid confirmed he was out. He wasn't breathing. I'd killed my first cat surgery patient on the very first day of my employment.

"That's it, damn it!" No more small animals in this practice, maybe forever." That promise was one I kept until seven years later when I vaccinated a friend's dog while on a farm call.

I made the necessary call to the owner, who turned out not to be the owner. The young man had no intention of paying to neuter a tomcat, let alone a dead one.

The story that he told me was that he'd found the cat alongside the road that morning and brought it in because the vet should know what to do with stray cats. Never the less, that poor kitty haunted me for years. What a way to start my first day!

It was a good thing there was so much need for vet work on cows, pigs, horses, and a new industry in Fort Recovery at that time, poultry. There simply wasn't enough time to take care of a small animal practice along with the demands of a large animal practice.

News of the young veterinarian killing his patient on his first day traveled fast in a small town. Gretta often spent hours gossiping on the party line. Much of the telephone service in Fort Recovery back then was on shared lines, so if you picked up the receiver and someone else was talking, it soon became multiple people participating in an unintended conference call.

It was plain and simple ease dropping, and it was probably the favorite recreational activity in town. Absolutely everyone heard the story with the adventure getting more interesting with each telling. Instead of being the new village idiot that I was, the stories made me into a hero of sorts.

"Doc Tebbe wrestled a huge bobcat that had rabies down by the Wabash River, and he didn't need to have the "mad dog disease" treatment because he had the shots when he was in vet school."

Well, at least they got the shots in vet school part right. Every vet student was vaccinated for rabies once a year while in veterinary college because the probability that each student would be exposed to rabies once in their career was one hundred percent.

The rest of the morning turned out pretty well. The next two farm calls were to treat cows for milk fever, a type of paralysis that happens after calving. All that's needed is an intravenous injection of a calcium solution that quickly relieved the cow's inability to get up.

Vaccinating pigs to prevent hog cholera was a large part of the income of the practice. On my first day, I had 272 pigs to inject with swine cholera serum at three farms.

That may sound like a lot of animals to treat, but this was such a common procedure perfected over the years that it took only a few seconds and it was on to the next one.

Lunch was forgotten because I was running behind schedule. The three little pigs were still in their burlap bag waiting for me back at the clinic.

A farmer who came in to pick up a couple of gallons of an electrolyte solution offered to hold the pigs while I performed the castration and repaired their hernias. A swab with iodine to the incision and a penicillin injection finished the surgery. My helper made a joke about a tomcat, so it looked like our Gretta told him of my fiasco.

The pig owner's car was still in the shade, but soon the hot summer sun would be shining on the pigs. We put the pigs back in their sack and sprinkled water on the bag to help keep the pigs cool.

About a minute later, Jeb, the owner of the pigs, came from the saloon a block away. He was having a hard time staying on the sidewalk. My helper, Lee said, "You're about to meet the town drunk. Good luck."

I had no idea the pigs belonged the town drunk. Jeb looked perfectly sober when he was in earlier.

A lot happened in my last four hours. Now, the pigs were in better shape than Jeb was. Jeb Hauser got drunk in those same four hours. He could do one thing at a time, and he did it very deliberately. Jeb fumbled for his keys and finally found them in the ignition. Then he said, "Thanks. Charge it" and proceeded to make a U-turn in front of a semi-truck. The air brakes hissed and the horn blared, but Jeb made his turn and left town with three pigs in the rumble seat. I was waiting for them to pop up and scream, "Please save us!!"

Gretta was not happy. She grumbled something about the charge for the pigs should be more so it would at least be as much as Jeb's bar bill.

Zandy was having a better day. After meeting with the Superintendent of the Fort Recovery School District, she was hired to teach the fourth grade at the elementary school. The school was within walking distance from the upstairs apartment we just rented.

"When are you coming home?" Zandy asked for the first time in the thousands during the following years. We settled for going to Thobe's Restaurant. We both had a long day and walked the couple blocks to the diner, and after a hearty meal of their specialty, meatloaf dinner, Zandy rode with me on the last two farm calls for the day.

She liked the people we met at the restaurant and the two farms, especially the two fourth-graders that were going to be in her classroom when school started in September.

It was a long day, but there was mostly satisfaction and a good feeling that we both had made the right decision in coming to Fort Recovery. We both felt that our professions were going to serve the community for a long time.

CONTAGION

Heavy footsteps clomping up the stairs to our second-floor apartment on Wayne Street in Fort Recovery was not my favorite way to wake up in a hurry. It wasn't quite five o'clock in the morning.

Mitch Brinkman introduced himself as he pushed the door to our bedroom open while I was still trying to find my pants. I wondered why I hadn't bought a gun to protect ourselves from criminal intruders. Mitch was bellowing something about millions of turkeys and chickens already dead and the end of the world being upon us!

Mitch was one of the field service specialists overseeing the animals and poultry that one of the feed mills in town serviced. Mitch was very competent at his work. I considered Mitch friend and a joy to work with on difficult problems.

In his hands were eight or ten good-sized turkeys in a bag, all of them dead. The grower called Mitch very early that morning and reported a chilling story of twenty thousand turkeys that were healthy the day before and now all that were left were reduced to a couple hundred very sick birds.

The ones in the garbage bag were still alive twenty minutes earlier, but now, they all were dead. "I don't think there will be any left by noon," Mitch said.

Mitch dropped the sack of dead birds at the foot of my bed and was already washing his hands so he could make coffee. My head was still wondering what just happened and Mitch was making coffee in my kitchen!

Zandy just pulled the covers over her head. With any luck, she would get another two hours of sleep.

often renders the organism less dangerous. In this instance, the bacteria went rogue, and now was threatening to wipe out millions of turkeys

This time it mutated in a threatening manner. This process of serial passage was responsible for some runaway infections through history. Bubonic Plague is an example of how catastrophic a disease introduced in this fashion can be. Thank goodness this bacterium turned out to be a weakling mutant and it didn't affect carrier animals and other birds than turkeys and also chickens to a lesser degree.

The people at Virginia Tech advanced the idea that an immune system approach could help. They created a bacterin consisting of killed disease organisms from our original samples and incorporated the bacterin in whey blocks.

Four semi trucks delivered the whey blocks about three days later. The milk product with the killed Pasteurella bacterin was available to every chicken and turkey in the area left alive.

Nobody predicted that this would be a cure, but it was just that. The end came ten days after that morning visit. More than two million birds died in those ten days.

The amazing thing was not one human or other animal got sick from the bacteria. Forty-five years later, I still think we were lucky.

VIEWPOINT ROAD

Viewpoint was just a junction of three roads in the countryside about four miles southeast of Fort Recovery. There are so many memories of that road and the little settlement of some of the most gifted people I have ever met.

First, let's talk about the road. It was a four-mile long, winding, squirrely dirt road that was paved just before I came to Fort Recovery. Since my road in front of our new home ended on Viewpoint Road, this was the road I traveled at least ten times a day going to and from seeing many of our clients.

It was also the most dangerous road in the county. When the county finally paved the road it did not make it any safer. In fact, it sparked the interest of most of the teenagers in town, who used it as a racetrack.

There was a better way to describe what the road was really like. At forty miles an hour, it was a pleasant and scenic drive through the countryside. At seventy -five and even up to a hundred miles an hour it was an adrenaline popping experience that if you survived, bragging rights were worth it.

Add underage alcohol drinking and it's no wonder that far too many fatal accidents happened on that four-mile stretch, not to mention many serious injuries.

Driving fast was one of my bad habits, but never on Viewpoint road, although the night a barn owl flew through my windshield the speedometer was probably registering a little faster than forty, not much.

The owl was flying visual on the centerline about three feet above the pavement. Surely the bird was going to get out of the way, but there was no change his flight pattern, and he hit my windshield headfirst. There was a loud pop on impact, followed with the bird flopping next to me on the seat. Feathers and glass crumbles covered everything inside the car.

It was chaos for a few minutes. The owl never knew what happened. My windshield had a hole about a half-inch in diameter. How did that relatively large bird squeeze through the little hole? A lot went through my shocked brain in those few seconds.

Later, the guy who fixed my windshield explained that the glass was flexible. The bird stretched the opening enough to pass through; then the hole closed up.

Sorry bird, you should have pulled up, I've felt bad about that bird incident for a long time and haven't told anybody until now. I was fairly sure people would have a hard time believing a barn owl could fit through a half inch hole in a windshield.

As a vet making farm calls, it wasn't rare for me to log a couple of hundred miles a day. I got pretty comfortable driving those old dusty farm roads once I learned to slow down for kids, dogs, deer, school buses, and owls.

Two of my favorite superheroes lived in the community of Viewpoint, and they lived next door to each other. They were brothers. One was a member of the group that saw the wisdom of guiding the agriculture future of the area. His name was Norb Mindson, and he led the agricultural and business people of the Fort Recovery area into an agricultural paradigm shift.

The applied business change brought partnerships with farmers, bankers, and the markets for the finished products. They worked together in a close bond to bring finished farm products to the consumer.

Watching that idea grow and flourish in Fort Recovery was wondrous. There was a name for that movement. It was called vertical integration. Years ago, before they had created this alliance in Fort Recovery, I was assigned a college journalism project on this subject. Several national farm magazines published my article. You can only imagine how amazing it was to see that idea working so well in the real world, years later.

Not everything was so perfect in the Fort Recovery agricultural world. There were setbacks. A flock of 20,000 hens owned by Norb died within twelve hours from Avian Influenza, with no survivors. A catastrophe like this was a reminder that farming was a risky business, and that there was a need for veterinary services. Sometimes those services got pretty messy.

As veterinarians, we were in charge of the cleanup, which was a big deal. In our favor was the host/virus relationship. Wild bird carriers probably introduced the airborne virus to the chickens. We found dead starlings and pigeons that got into the laying house before they died.

Lab results showed they were avian influenza virus victims. The virus killed the carrier birds very quickly, and in doing so, both the wild bird group and the chickens also died suddenly. They were all lying dead within a closed laying house. The only relatively good thing about their deaths was there were no birds alive to allow the virus to replicate further. The flu virus had a very short lifespan outside the sick live birds. It did not live and multiply in dead birds.

The hard work was removing dead chickens from cages holding ten birds each cage. This task was done by hand, and the workers were mainly under twenty. They were naturally worried that this virus disease might infect people.

The CDC (Center for Disease Control) assured us that this particular strain that was so disastrous to the birds was the human flu virus. The virus was harmless to humans because people have been getting vaccinated for this strain for decades and have built up immunity to this virus. The vaccine stopped it in people, and in time, immunization with the old human strain would give the same results for chickens.

Another family that managed a poultry business for as long as anyone living in the Fort Recovery area can remember was the Klincern family. In the sixties, a family member who at that time was old, tired, and in bad shape managed the chicken farm and feed mill. He had died of heart disease before I got to know him. A young nephew and his bride from Charleston, West Virginia were dispatched to take over the family business. Tim and Martie became fast friends of Zandy and myself.

The first task after their arrival was to clean out the old house so they could move in. During the cleanup process, Tom took much of the furniture to the town landfill. The next day the landfill custodian called to let Tim know that his uncle had a big collection of old coins stuffed into the legs

Fast Cars and Gravel Roads

There has always been an association of fast cars and gravel roads as a concept of how dangerous these roads were in rural Ohio fifty years ago. Maybe we should spend some time describing how people moved about in those times.

Rural Mercer County in the Fort Recovery area had good roads for the time. Paved county roads connected all the small hamlets and the wider state highways connected all the towns. Narrow graded limestone gravel roads were the other eighty-five percent. . Crushed limestone was cheap and easily accessible. Boy-oh-Boy, could you do some crazy burn outs on that gravel!

The township trustees maintained these gravel roads in their neighborhoods pretty well. The significant problem was that all these roads were too narrow to accommodate the new wider and heavier cars and trucks Detroit was turning out. The county roadways and bridges could not keep up with the needs of the new automobiles people wanted

During the 50's, high school excitement centered on pretty girls and awesome muscle cars. Unfortunately, the cars were affordable for families of hot-blooded teenagers. Speed and under-aged drinking resulted in too many highway fatalities in the State of Ohio. By far, most deaths occurred on the narrow gravel roads.

I grew up on a farm with one of those narrow gravel roads. It was so narrow it was impossible for me to negotiate a borrowed Indian motorcycle through the piled loose gravel in the middle of the road. One Sunday afternoon, I carelessly swerved to end up in a painful, bloody skid. It also ended the expectation of ever putting my butt on the seat of a motorcycle for the rest of my life.

When I was about thirteen back on the farm, we had a colorful veterinarian that I idolized. Just west of our farm buildings and the fruit orchard was a substantial depression in our road. That dip apparently fascinated our vet, Dr. Vernon Steinke.

This man drove faster than any person in the county. He also drank more whiskey than anyone in the county. In spite of all this and wrecking several cars a year, he was considered an excellent veterinarian.

Of course, at thirteen, most boys thought the vet's bold and vigorous character was pretty cool. We all thought that's what we wanted to be a fast driving, hard drinking vet when we grew up. What a role model! I did later become a vet and was known in the same county to have a lead foot, but never took to the spirits much.

One hot summer day when I was fifteen, I went to our neighbor to use her party line telephone to call the veterinarian to look at our pigs. The pigs were not doing well in the summer heat. Two mature pigs had already died, and some of the others were breathing hard and fast. It was terrifying to a kid like me who didn't like to see an animal die!

The days were dry and hot, something that pigs didn't tolerate very well. Pigs don't sweat, so they usually cooled off by plopping in a convenient mud hole.

Our road was washboard and very dusty even without a hot, dry spell. On that day we called for Dr. Steinke's help with the pigs, a dust cloud churned and lingered long after anybody drove by. No matter how slow a car moved, it still set off a small storm of dust.

Dr. Steinke never drove slowly. He made a huge dust cloud! The dusty rooster-tail rose hundreds of feet above the road and followed close behind the vet's gray Oldsmobile. For some crazy reason, he was racing his car at a hundred miles an hour over the narrow gravel road that was treacherous at thirty.

We heard the noise of his coming before we saw him. The sound made us feel like something awful was about to happen. There was no way he was going to be able to stop at our place. If he would still be going that fast at the next intersection, he would have to squeeze through a narrow steel bridge at an angle. That probably was not going to happen.

The oppressive heat, the noise, and immense dust cloud spearheaded by a gray automobile driven by our vet were ominous. The vet looked like he was right out of "Back to the Future"; driving like a drunk, bat out of Hell. Not something a fifteen-year-old kid should see!

The vet roared past the chicken coop where I was gathering the eggs. The road dropped into a steep but short dip just past the chicken house. The cloud of dust made vision impossible to place a picture to the horrible noise.

Suddenly there was no noise from the car for a second or two until he came down from his airborne launch and hit the other side of the dip crosswise, then skidded through the ditch and took out three hundred feet of fence.

Incredibly the car was still slamming and banging its way across our neighbor's pasture field. There was too much dust to see what Dr. Steinke was doing out there.

Dr. Steinke turned the newly wrinkled Olds back through the hole in the fence and drove back into our barnyard, looking normal and ready to go to work. "I always wanted to take that dip at a "hunnert," he calmly exclaimed. We all stood and looked at him with our mouths open. This guy was plum crazy! My dad laughed nervously and said, "Glad you made it Doc. On a serious note, our pigs are mighty sick, and we need your help".

Dr. Steinke looked at the pigs for a minute and told my dad that the pigs were hot and dehydrated and that they weren't drinking enough water, probably because it was dirty. We were told to get some clean troughs and water them four to five times a day, especially on hot days. He sold us a case of four gallons of an electrolyte solution that smelled like a candy factory. Then he cleaned his boots and was gone.

"Wow! What a man!" was my impression. He was like a pre-modern day Dukes of Hazard. Character The next afternoon at our FFA meeting at the Ag shop there would be a lot of bragging about what happened down our crazy dirt road.

Poor boys like me never grew up to be a vet like Dr. Steinke, but we can dream.

The orders Dr, Steinke gave to my father turned into a full day of cleaning a dirty pigpen, shoveling a ton of pig manure and making water troughs out of wood planks.

We had no money to buy new metal water troughs, nor did we have enough to pay for the medicine Dr. Steinke sold us. My father was not able to hold back the tears. My dad was a proud, honest and intelligent man, but we were poor!

The next morning, all the pigs and sows were sick. We didn't have to call a vet to know our entire hog population of one hundred and three animals would be dead in three days from hog cholera. My father knew it was cholera. He had lived through it several times.

We depended on selling pigs at the market to be our ticket out of poverty and near despair. Our hopes for a brighter future disappeared. Every one of our pigs died.

My whole family didn't smile for days. We knew we would have another hard year with no money. After this, I forgot any thoughts of being a veterinarian. The only thing the vet left us was a bill for the electrolytes, and 300 feet of torn fence that we had to repair before the neighbor's small herd found the hole.

The worst chore ever was to dig a trench to bury the dead pigs, carry them to the trench as they died, and cover them with lime, then soil. We were one grieving family for the next several days of the most miserable days of our lives. I had a name for every one of those pigs, big and small.

We made it through the brutal winter that year. We were fortunate to have cows to feed the family instead of a couple of pigs that year. The cows still gave milk to sell, and we ate a lot of chickens and everything that grew in our huge garden and put up in glass jars, so we didn't starve. I sure did miss my pigs.

The next year was our first year attempting to raise tomatoes. Our twenty acres of tomatoes produced more money than we dreamed it would. The tomatoes were ripening three weeks early before the canning company accepted the tomato crop.

We picked hampers of bright, beautiful tomatoes and loaded from forty to a hundred containers on the wagon early in the morning; It depended on how many ripe tomatoes we could pick the day before. We then drove the tractor and wagon to Celina fourteen miles away. There we sold every tomato door-to-door almost every day for those three weeks.

We were proud of our tomatoes and for good reasons. In the stores, a three-day-old hothouse tomato sold for a quarter apiece. We sold our hampers of thirty large fresh vine-ripened fresh tomatoes for a dollar! Every house bought at least one hamper.

One of my FFA projects that year was to plant a relatively small field to raise tomatoes as a cash crop. Our vocational agriculture advisor showed us how to manage farm projects and keep records on everything.

There were a test and a grade for the project at the end of the year. Also, we entered our record books in a state competition. As a sophomore, my project won the field project for the state that year.

Ironically, because of all the limestone dust that we hated so much, from the road next to the tomatoes, actually helped to balance the pH of the soil. The cloud from the road seemed to give us a bigger, bumper crop than ever.

My high school activities consisted of my FFA projects and learning there was a big world out there. Studying and homework did not take up much of my time, but books were another matter. I could read an entire history textbook in two or three days. This ability was not bad considering I taught myself to read when I was twelve.

It was strange how that happened. It wasn't until the sixth grade that reading class changed from nothing but the teacher reading children's books to the class to learning to read, thanks to a better teacher.

Thanks also to being a Mass server, I could read Latin before I learned to read English. Five years were enough of "Uncle Wiggly"!

Our family lived so far from the high school that participating in athletic programs was not possible; not to mention there were endless chores we all had. The bus ride time was two and a half hours, twice a day. That's when I studied novels, classics, and the encyclopedia. During my free time I devoured books; any book I could get. During study hall for four years, I volunteered to be the student librarian.

We scraped enough money together to buy a Holstein heifer from the proceeds of the door-to-door tomato sales. She was growing into a beautiful animal. I was planning to show her at the county fair as my dairy project for my second FFA project.

The heifer, Shirley won Grand Champion at the county fair, probably because I slept in her stall all week, I loved that girl. I was going to be the president of the Coldwater FFA Chapter next year and was living a young farm boy's dream. Being a farmer someday in the future wasn't looking like a bad choice for me, no doubt about it!

Eighteen months later my heifer Shirley was now called a cow because she was going to have a calf. My dad called me to the barn early one November morning. Shirley was in labor and was having trouble. The calf was just too big for her to deliver it without help. I felt helpless watching my sweet Shirley struggle. My dad was doing all he could. My sister ran to the neighbor's house to call Dr. Steinke for help since we still didn't have telephone service.

He was there within minutes. He looked at the situation and went to his car to get a lot of equipment, then ordered three buckets of warm water with towels. He told me to get out of the barn. Of course, I went up to the next floor and watched from a hay chute. That was my cow, and I wasn't going anywhere.

The calf was stuck, and after pulling with a come along for what seemed like an eternity, he stopped. Next thing, to my horror he started cutting off legs, head, and ribs. He yelled to nobody, probably to himself, "I hate to do this, but it's our only chance to save the cow." Soon my calf and cow were both dead, and the vet had finally stopped his frantic butchering.

Dr. Steinke had a breakdown, complete with shouting, pounding the dead cow with his fists, and cussing. Suddenly, he picked up all his equipment and carried it to the car, no explanation, and no apology. He tore out of the driveway the same way he came in. I was eighteen years and one day old when my cherished Shirley died.

It broke my heart. My reaction for years was anger. I could not believe the butchery and cruelty. From that day forward, the thought prevailed that being a veterinarian would give me the chance to show that I could be a better veterinarian than Dr. Steinke. I wanted to make up for what he did to my Shirley!

Ten years later I was a newly hatched D.V.M. with a big job ahead of me. I had to find a way to dump the weight of anger; the baggage I had carried far too long. That feeling of failure and frustration on the day that Shirley died would spur me to make sure I was skilled at cesarean surgery so that I would never have to watch a cow and calf die needlessly again.

As veterinarians, we felt that the animals we treat were somehow our own, so we had a vested interest in their lives and the lives of their families.

I had colossal failures myself along the way that made me realize how bad Dr. Steinke must have felt in those moments when he realized he could not save my Shirley. The anger had finally dissipated; replaced by sympathetic understanding for a comrade who chose a demanding profession; a profession where you did the best you could with the knowledge and the tools available, and knowing no matter how hard you try there will be a few souls lost along the way.

This understanding came with a big dose of humility that kept me on track for a very long time. The learning curve on how to perform cesarean sections was a little rough at first, but as time passed, it became my favorite surgery.

Through the fifty years or more, there was only one situation that indicated the need for dismembering a calf. Incredibly, before that happened, the cow delivered the "monster calf " without any help. I delivered hundreds, maybe thousands of calves through the years but never had to dismember even one.

In honor of Dr. Steinke, driving fast and hard to get to the next emergency call became my habit also, and when there was no emergency, it still felt good to drive fast.

MONSTER

Every veterinarian in practice for ten years has stories of animals born with serious genetic defects. Sometimes, the client like Don Feckler remembered the event more vividly. Certainly my rendition of the baby calf born in his barn was tame compared to what he remembered.

Don Feckler saw the Devil dancing in the rafters the day one of his cows gave birth to a schistostroma reflexus achrondroplastic bull calf weighing about eighty pounds (Sorry to describe the condition this way, but a description like this is more terrifying than using plain English and these creatures were certainly spooky).

Don was one of my favorite clients to visit, but like everybody, he had his faults. The major fault was that he never paid his veterinary bills. While he owed relatively a modest sum per invoice, the dates of the older invoices went back more than five years.

Other than that, Don was a nice enough gentleman who read classics and took good care of his herd of thirty milk cows. His cows consisted of several breeds. Most notably, he was a very good cook. A bachelor, never married, he was a graduate of a very well known school of theology. His sudden change from Army Chaplin to farmer took place when he was discharged at the end of the Korean War. He was a few years older than I was.

His farm was nestled in the moraine hills of east central Indiana. It was a long trip, especially for an emergency call. On previous visits it was common for Don to have a home baked fruit pie with ice cream and black coffee at the house. We talked about the books each of us was reading at the time.

His interest had noticeably changed in his choice of books. History themes made a shift to a fascination of the books of preference being Edgar Allen Poe, Richard Matheson's, "I Am Legend" and Henry James', "The Turning of the Screw," a ghost story.

He quizzed me about my belief in ghosts, and strangely he wanted to know everything I knew about communicable diseases.

On this sunny August afternoon there was no time for friendly nonsense. From his voice on the telephone there was intense fear in his plea, "Come as quickly as you can. I am really scared!" Frankly, he scared me as well; particularly since he gave me no idea what had frightened him.

Upon arrival, he met me with, "It's Dark Lady. She is in the maternity pen and I have hot water and towels for you. She has something strange coming out of her back end."

Dark Lady was an older Holstein cow of good quality, but the calf head sticking out with no front feet in sight was truly ugly scary. It was a "bulldog calf" with all the lethal genetic traits. The confused genetics corrupted the way fetal development is supposed to progress.

In this case, that development went seriously haywire. The black grotesque head was a good 30% of the weight of the calf. Its eyes were huge, bulging, and rolling back and forth, seeing nothing. The mouth was malformed with the lower jaw protruding with an oversized tongue lolling back and forth.

Even for a seasoned vet, who I wasn't yet, this was a gruesome sight. The poor thing had a horrible screaming, grunt; it was so eerie and shocking. I could barely hear Don struggling to speak over the calf's cries.

I went right to work and paid little attention to Don. The delivery looked like a challenge. My excruciating job would be when the calf would finally be delivered alive. I would have to inject a lethal dose of euthanasia solution as quickly as I could so the calf's suffering would come to an end.

I was reaching into the birth canal to straighten the front legs so I could pull the calf out. Just as I got them straight, the realization that we were dealing with something a lot more serious than we could ever think of, became clear. I had the beating heart of the bulldog calf in my hand!

Don retreated into a corner in the fetal position, shaking and muttering very strange sounds and speaking in tongues interrupted only by some easy to distinguish simple prayers. It was getting worse. Soon he was on the straw bedding, going into convulsions. Ministering aid to the client now became the immediate priority. Lady, the cow finished the delivery without my help.

Don went through spasms repeatedly and finally stopped, but his eyeballs were still looking at his cranium. It was imperative to move him from the stable with the poor deformed monster because what came out last was the really gross stuff.

During final stages of fetal development, normally the skin closed completely around the body and connected from the sternum to the pubis. Since the cow stands on four feet, that area would be the entire chest and belly. In this case that skin never covered the front, exposing the lungs and heart from the chest and all the viscera from the abdomen. The poor calf was inside out.

I humanely as possible euthanized the calf with an intravenous injection.

Don was doing kind of OK, so I finished cleaning up the stall and the cow. I wrapped the calf in a blanket from the office room and carried the calf out to the truck and closed the lid. There was enough time to clean up and dry off by the time Don came out of his trance.

Before he became aware of his surroundings, Don gave witness to his confession of all the sinful events of his life and promised his earnest efforts to be a better man.

It was nearly an hour after everything was done at the barn before it was safe to leave him. Don was in his house still shaking even wrapped in double blankets; shock on a warm summer day.

I stopped at his neighbor to tell them that Don might need some help for a couple of hours. I also told them what to expect and that he was going to be OK.

The next day I called him to see how he was doing and if Dark Lady was all right. I had a small present for his enjoyment I wanted to give him (and distraction from the previous day's terror and his spooky books).

Later that day when I got to his place, he greeted me quietly and offered his apology for anything he might have said, or if he had offended me. I said, "No, there is no problem, but I brought you a book I finished reading.

It's an early book by James Mitchner, called "Caravan," about Afghanistan after the Second World War. I thought you could be ready to start reading something other than scary horror novels.

He then handed me an envelope along with an invitation to join him at the old kitchen table for that delicious promised slice of apple pie, ice cream, and coffee.

Later, I opened the envelope in the truck to find a check for nearly three thousand dollars, enough to cover six years of past veterinary bills. I thought to myself, you are a good man Don Feckler.

AUTUMN 1964

Fort Recovery was an active place to live in the early Sixties. Almost everyone was German of some sort, everybody had a job, and the schools graduated bright young men and women. Most of these bright young men and women left town and became a part of Fort Recovery's most famous export.

Some went to war in a far-off place called Vietnam while others sought higher education and good jobs where they made good use of their strong work ethic.

The gifted athletes left, and more than a few did very well in professional sports. Few came back to make their lives in Fort Recovery; they only returned home for family reunions. After all, most came from large families, and there was no room for all of them on the farm.

For many years the only way for a young man to get out of town was if they joined the military, were a hotshot baseball player or became a priest. For women, it was even more daunting. That was beginning to change for the better.

In the space of a few years, the community needed skilled professional businessmen and women, teachers, doctors and veterinarians, nutritionists, agricultural engineers and high school coaches capable of leading the high school to state championships.

The businesses and Chamber of Commerce began an effort to recruit young professionals to come to Fort Recovery. Come they did; they came with their young families and skills to energize the community.

Immediately the town had an enthusiastic Jaycees Club, a Kiwanis Club, and Little League games filled the summer days. There was a community drive for lights at the park for adult softball and extended Little League games. We had a lot of talk about building a community pool. Constructing new homes were created for the first time in many years.

The Fort was a bona fide "Boom Town"! When Zandy and I decided to come to Fort Recovery to settle in, we had no idea what to expect. In a short time, the town exceeded all our expectations.

The main force stimulating this sleepy town was the ability of its hometown businessmen who recognized an opportunity in the productive agricultural output from the farmers in the area.

The land was fertile, but the potential of her stewards was even more so. Instead of exporting hundreds of thousands of tons of grain to the giant cereal companies, the area sought to export processed meat and eggs from poultry, market pigs, and feedlot cattle as finished market foods found in grocery stores.

Packaging centers were built, and a new poultry plant capable of processing several million turkeys and chickens, and a related packaging center added jobs for several hundred workers.

It was also the opportune time for the large animal veterinary professionals to change the way its members ought to serve the food animal industry. For several years the treatment of pets by veterinarians was successfully improving its services to bring the profession in line with what the people with pets wanted. Pet owners appreciated service and compassion.

In Vet school classes we were taught the principles of herd health management for food animal production instead of rushing from one emergency to the next. The challenge was that the "fire engine" practice was the entrenched model of practice, and that was what we would find in our new placements. It was up to us as the recent graduates to foster that movement, or not.

Animal health management had a long way to go to replace sick animal treatment practice. The Fort Recovery Veterinary Clinic was no exception. Indeed, we expected emergency calls to manage chaos as everyday events, but generally, the practitioners of the large animal health profession were not looking for prevention at the time. It was time for a paradigm shift. Boy! Was I ever ready to be a part of that movement!

The practice in Fort Recovery was not my first choice. My application for Veterinarian-in-Charge for a large dairy in Argentina didn't quite come through for me. I was the second choice from nearly a hundred veterinarians from around the world. A professor at Cornell University was their pick, and he accepted. After swallowing my pride from losing the high-profile glamorous position, the offer from Dr. Mitchner in my hometown looked like a perfect match. As it turned out, I couldn't be happier.

Dr. Mitchner's practice received its revenue mainly from vaccinating pigs for hog cholera. Within two years the US Department of Agriculture planned to stop injecting pigs with serum because it was the last obstacle in the eradication of this disastrous plague that for decades had been decimating the swine industry.

Thank goodness Dr. Mitchner was open-minded. He saw the change coming and already had a reputation of being the veterinarian to call regarding swine and poultry health management problems.

We discussed the change in our future practice direction shortly after he came back from his vacation. His interest grew as I explained what the role of this practice could be with a change toward preventive medicine. His only comment was. "Can you do it"? I answered, "You bet!" And he said, "Good. You're in charge. The practice can handle the cost of any changes we may have to make." We shook hands on the deal, and both of us never had any reason to have regrets.

True to his promise, Dr. Mitchner spent the money from the practice to move into a landmark structure of Fort Recovery, the State Line Tavern. Why would we want to buy a bar? Most important was that it was the only building for sale in town. The "For Sale" sign out front had been placed there eight years prior. Also, it had a good roof and a nice finish on the cement floor from gallons of beer spilled that aged well into a dark amber shine.

There was a small pond in back stocked with huge hybrid bluegill sunfish. Three fish would not fit into a ten-quart bucket. I wondered if this was where their fish dinners came from.

Anyhow, now we owned a bar, without the license, and the town only had six bars left. The place was ideal for a laboratory to diagnose diseases on chickens and turkeys. We needed a dry space to store medicines and nutritional pre-mixes. Our laboratory was well equipped for routine diagnostic procedures for our needs since both the states of Ohio and Indiana diagnostic labs were so far away. The building handily fulfilled all our needs.

We routinely performed an autopsy at no charge on every farm animal that died with an unknown diagnosis. We considered each time we performed an autopsy was an educational experience.

We did charge for poultry autopsies. For some reason, we called it a necropsy when it pertained to birds, but it's the same thing. We examined batches of sick birds and tissues cultured for bacteria, and then tested for which antibiotic would be most practical to treat.

The only piece of equipment that was a bad investment was an operating table for cows that needed their hooves trimmed while lying on the operating table.

It was easier to do this the old fashioned way of lifting the foot and trim the hooves much like the farrier trims feet on horses. Injuries and scrapes happened far more often to the veterinarians while using the operating table.

Local and systematic pain relieving procedures allowed us to do most of our large animal surgeries standing upright.

By the time the US Department of Agriculture put a stop on vaccinating pigs, we were already well into preventive health management for our poultry and those with food animals. Our business never missed the income from vaccinating pigs for cholera, but many traditional practices did. The government program was successful in that it stopped hog cholera disease.

The strongest service we supplied was nutritional advice. Our best tool was a large computer in the state agriculture college and the help it provided veterinarians managing computerized nutritionally balanced formulas for livestock.

Why should I be so enthusiastic about computers in 1964? Along with access to a university computer, we also had the input of some very helpful nutrition experts and companies that provided packaged micronutrients and trace minerals. In another ten years the first personal computer was introduced, so for a decade, the dairy industry was way out on the point of proper nutrition with their punch cards.

Monthly milk production records were tools to discuss with the dairyman the information collected and incorporated that into our management recommendations for how to feed the cows for maximum milk production.

Our breeding selection program was applied to every cow inseminated by artificial breeding, a program very familiar to me, having spent several years as an artificial insemination technician.

There was a lot to deliver regarding management help, and with the promise of, "If we cannot help fix your problems, you don't owe us," the programs got off to a fast start. Not a single dairyman showed dissatisfaction once they got used to being charged for veterinary services not considered just a year earlier.

There was no better stimulation than profit, and the dairies quickly cooperated.

A disclaimer is owed concerning how it was possible for a new veterinarian recently out of vet school with the confidence to pass as an expert on dairy herd production. That was my part time job for six years while attending undergraduate and vet school at the University. Before that, my first real job was being an artificial breeding technician. My second job was several years as an Army field medic.

That work through college was also the reason for being caught napping in my eight O'clock warm classrooms. Getting up at four AM, conducting dairy milk production testing and records made an eight o'clock nap feel like heaven.

Also, many weekends were spent substituting for neighboring artificial breeding technicians. My part-time jobs throughout six years of college were mostly related to working with dairy cows. I received my 10,000 cow pin while in vet school (10,000 successful artificial insemination. conceptions which was a surprise) Time flies when you're happily busy, somehow adding up to be the second oldest graduate in the Class of 1962 at twenty-eight years of age.

The farmer-veterinarian bond was strong in the agricultural lands of America. A veterinarian who was genuinely interested in contributing his or her knowledge to help a dairyman friend with real problems presented a powerful opportunity for problem solving. Talk among good friends got down to business quickly as a matter of what the farmer's problems are and his expectations, answered by the veterinarian who lists what he or she can do concerning professional skills.

The price of the professional expertise was always negotiable. Sometimes our best advice was to refer technical help like milking machine vendors or professional nutritionists to address the heart of some of the most challenging situations.

As vets, our continuing education included a lot more than clinical practice. We understood the business of our client. We also were the local expert on nutrition, genetics, animal physiology, diseases, and business records.

Fortunately, the American Association of Bovine Practitioners featured one such topic in depth every year at its conventions. Topics included genetics, nutrition, mastitis management, and understanding the information hidden in monthly production reports.

To be a speaker at these conferences was more than an honor. It also included expenses for travel, room, registration, plus a stipend for preparation and presentation.

Since there weren't many bovine practitioners involved in preventive medicine both Dr. Mitchner and I appeared on the speaker's list for a few years. Dr. Mitchner presented topics concerning the poultry industry while I spoke only about dairy production.

Dr. Mitchner met Dr. Lyle Baker from California, at one of these conferences, and convinced him to visit our practice in Ohio. Dr. Baker was the prominent leader in the changing focus of food animal veterinary management. His input on our preventive medicine application made all the difference.

With time, veterinarians from colleges replaced us with their better vocabulary and delivery; thus more intelligent, I suppose. It took me a long time to realize these new guys were indeed smarter than me.

Ten years later Doctor Hungate presented a great seminar at the Bovine Practitioner Conference in 1974 on the functions of ruminant animal digestion. (In case you lost me in the matter of time, we just jumped ten years!)

The seminar lasted three days, ten hours a day in San Francisco. The information took away the mystery of how an animal like a cow could eat grass and make thousands of gallons of milk out the other end. We also talked about the thousands of pounds of manure that came out the other end as well.

That information explained to a dairy farmer had two good outcomes; first, the vet appeared very smart if he kept his facts straight, and second, understanding even a little of how a rumen works as opposed to a stomach digesting food was the key for better nutrition and respect for their differences.

After an intellectual presentation by Dr. Hungate, the veterinarians in the audience finally were exposed to the scientific facts needed to apply in their practices. It felt like a humbling moment hit me; I wasn't as smart as I thought. It made sense to be satisfied to remain a student from there on.

There is a saying that goes, "To discover that to learn what you didn't know is a gift to the student. To apply what you just learned from the master is the greatest gift the teacher could wish for." Thank you, Dr. Hungate.

That veterinary conference had another significant moment in my life. I had the good fortune to meet Mr. James Wight, better known as James Herriot, the well-read veterinarian/author from the Yorkshire Dales in the U.K.

The program for the Bovine Practitioner's Conference activities list regarding things to see off sites for the families included the opportunity to buy his new release, "All things Bright and Beautiful" and have it signed by James Herriot at a book signing event at Macy's in downtown San Francisco.

I didn't go because I wanted to absorb everything discussed on the rumen digestion topic by Dr. Hungate. Dr. Baker did go to the book signing with a mission in mind. I mentioned Dr. Lyle Baker often in my stories as my mentor with all things preventive medicine and a good friend. I never knew what he would do next, and that Sunday was no exception.

Dr. Baker and his wife Barbara entered the large space reserved for this very famous writer. The room was full of James Herriot's fans to the point of being uncomfortable. Without hesitation, Dr. Baker went to the desk where James Herriot was signing books and takes in the situation. Apparently, the process was quite slow, with not only signing the inside cover, but James Herriot was also writing long phrases that used both pages.

The author was fatigued and claustrophobic according to his comments later that evening. Dr. Baker said to him, 'How would you like to meet some real men?" The two men had known each other for several years.

The event coordinator was persuaded to give James Herriot a ten-minute break. I never knew what conspired in those ten minutes, but with the help of Dr. Baker, the two men signed about 200 books in three hours.

There were two versions of how they accomplished the feat we heard later in the evening. One by James Herriot said that Dr. Baker sat at another desk and prepped the book owner on what to say and then passed the patron on to him to sign.

The other version was from the wife of one of the veterinarians at the book signing who said that Dr. Baker sat at a desk around a corner and passed himself as James Herriot, signing her book as James Herriot. Although there was a remarkable similarity in the features of both men – except height, she knew Lyle Baker. She then went over to the desk where James Herriot was signing to get him to sign it; He signed it, "Lyle Baker D.V.M." This lady showed me the book with both signatures, and they were identical. I would bet that Lyle Baker signed at least half the books that afternoon.

The mixing with the veterinarians after the sessions was quite casual. The conference was at the Continental Mark Hopkins and the huge bar called the "Top of the Mark" was the after-meeting place where the veterinarians gathered to swap lies - and drink.

Dr. Baker inserted himself into the group, along with another man he introduced as Dr. Wight from the U.K. I didn't recognize the name and it seemed, neither had anybody else. I never heard of Dr. James Wight, but I did know that in the British Isles, a veterinarian is addressed as "Mister" as opposed to "Doctor" because I read that in "All Creatures Large and Small".

The group of bovine practitioners meeting at nine o'clock in the bar associated with the conference was a tradition. It was a meeting place to catch up with old friends around the country. At some point, the topic morphed into a liars club, and almost everyone had a chance to participate. That group had at least thirty veterinarians in lively conversations.

Dr. Wight (AKA, James Herriot) was thoroughly enjoying himself, making friends and swapping stories. It was impossible not to notice his chipped English diction and quaint way of describing his home country. "I don't live in England. I live in the lovely Yorkshire Dales" he answered to the question of, "Where in England do you live?

At that point, Dr. Baker introduced his guest as James Herriot and handed him a microphone. For the next hour, James Herriot had the stage. It was non-stop delightful stories of animals and people, comments from the audience, lots of questions and answers, and eventually, mule stories by the vets.

There had to be several hundred people standing or scattered at full booths and tables. It was already past midnight, and the bar was scheduled to close at 2 O'clock. Most of the early group of vets gave up their chairs to accommodate a new group with new stories, lies and what it is that they like about being a veterinarian. James Herriot was one of the last to leave.

For some reason, writing a book someday took purchase in my mind and never left.

APRIL 11, 1965
THE PALM SUNDAY TORNADO DISASTER

There are dates in our lives that burn scars in our memories. In a sleepy community like Fort Recovery, one would think that not much happened there. The Jaycees social party the night before was the most exciting thing to happen in months. The mixer was a means to introduce all the young men and their wives and girlfriends to each other.

The young women graced the event as only beautiful young ladies can. The Jaycees had dancing, a potluck and a bit of drinking, but not much.

For Zandy and me, it was our first real local social event in three years and I didn't want to make a fool of myself. There was little chance of that for me; duty called and I missed the whole event.

Brother Bernie at the St. Charles Seminary dairy farm had an emergency call concerning one of their cows delivering twins, just before we were going to leave the house. The Brothers delivered one Brown Swiss calf, but the second calf was too much for them. Friends Jim and Paula took Zandy to the dance for me, and as it turned out, they brought her home as well.

Brother Bernie let me know that it would be miserable with the rain and that they had a large tent set up so we at least wouldn't drown. A quick change into work clothes and coveralls probably would keep me from getting pneumonia.

The dystocia was particularly difficult. The twins ended up as triplets and the cow was temporarily paralyzed from pressure caused by the twisted calf's leg pinching a major nerve trunk inside the pelvis. Trying to pull harder only made things worse.

The second calf was somehow turned sideways. This was a first for me to have this kind of dystocia and I immediately started to think of performing a cesarean section. First, I should at least try to find a leg, then the second leg. The maneuver worked, and from positioning, then to twisting the calf 180 degrees, the torsion (twist) unwound and we had plenty of room to pull the calf out.

The Brothers must have said several Rosaries for the calf because she beat the odds of not surviving. After a difficult delivery, the cow usually received a capsule of sulfa deep into the uterus. That's when I found the third calf tucked into one of the uterine horns, It was dead and shriveled so it had died weeks ago. There was no infection. The cow was beginning to get some feeling in her rear legs so her prognosis was pretty good. If she needed intravenous calcium later, the Brothers could handle it.

After Sunday morning Mass I drove over to pick up Jim, who previously asked if he could ride with me in the morning if a call came up. I just received a call to help a cow in dystocia south of Portland, Indiana. It was Palm Sunday and the weather was unseasonably warm and threatening to rain. The radio forecast included a severe weather alert.

At nine O'clock in the morning, it was unusually dark due to the heavy cloud cover. The sky was a single dark cloud with not a hint of a breeze. That's a pretty close description of how Jim looked. He evidentially had a beer or more after the dance when the party gravitated to Meinerding's Tavern. The beer was to wash down the main course of chicken livers and gizzards; the "Fort's Fad" at the time.

Since Jim was a pillar of professionalism, he probably had too many gizzards and livers and wasn't feeling very well but he was well enough to accompany me on a call to deliver a calf.

We talked about the Jaycees club and some of the events he was involved in as a member of The 20's & 30's Club in Missouri before they moved to Fort Recovery. We hoped that the good experiences some of the members in other organizations had in other parts of the country could be incorporated in our new Jaycees Club.

The lane at the farm was too muddy to chance getting stuck so we parked on a knoll populated by an old stand of hickory trees. Jim asked if

When the storm hit Lynn, we were back home; completely unaware of the devastation only twenty miles from where we were on our farm call.

The Jaycees of Fort Recovery, Ohio had their first community project even before they were organized. All twenty-five members spent from two to ten days at the devastated town and nearby farms. Those who had tractors, front-end loaders and bulldozers worked day and night removing victims and clearing the wreckage. There was little to tear down. The town was flat; blown away!

The town was, and still is Lynn, Indiana. As a neighbor village of Fort Recovery, many residents gave days and weeks of volunteering to help rebuild the town. Six of the Fort Recovery Jaycees were put to work searching for bodies, along with a small army of volunteers from all over Ohio and Indiana. Our group went until we dropped, logging fifty-four hours of digging without sleep. On Wednesday morning, the last missing person was accounted for. One-eighth of the population of Lynn was injured.

The people from that part of the country were no strangers to the devastation following forces of nature. They mourned, they rebuilt, and they found strength and resolve to carry on because this was home.

Not everyone had that resolve. After a tornado struck the area there were families who had enough scares by tornados and they moved away, usually far away to a place safer.

On the little farm where the calf was delivered, the mother cow and her baby were the only survivors. Eight other cows were killed in the smaller, freakish storm.

Tornado Lynn Indiana
weather.gov

THIS OLD BARN IS HOT WIRED

Fort Recovery has been a dense farming area since the 1830s as evidenced by parts of houses and barns that still reveal pieces of original construction. Additions were made through the years, as more space was needed.

In 1835 a barn protected about four cows and six workhorses on an eighty-acre farm. A hundred years later in 1936 the country was still in a deep depression, so there was little change.

It wasn't until the end of World War II and the return of the soldiers that changed everything. College education was offered to the veterans and soon educated farmers embraced new concepts of agriculture. Farmers still milked their cows by hand, but that was changing with the use of milking machines. Families grew, and so did the demand for clean, healthy milk.

Herd size grew to where one man could milk thirty cows without hired help. The farmers had to enlarge their too small barns around the original structure. Comfortable, free stall beds kept the cows cleaner and easier to milk. Ten more years brought us up to the late 50's and 60's, the age of technology regarding machinery and ideas.

Nobody milked cows by hand in 1960. The herds tripled in size in Ohio, so the barns adjusted to the new paradigm. New technology, included building design brought more features added to the original old barn. That is when I came on the scene as a young veterinarian. Within six months every barn within twenty-five miles became my workspace.

Those old barns with long wide beams from ancient trees, hand hewn with an adze and held together with wooden pegs were immensely sturdy. Beams often measured twenty inches squared and as long as the barn, often up to fifty feet long. By the 1960's those beams were valuable for furniture. They came from well-seasoned black walnut, ash, oak, and often, chestnut trees. The value of a single chestnut beam was enough to build a modern barn in some cases. With prices like that, the old barns began to disappear.

In 1936, Electricity came to the farm by way of the Rural Electrification Act. It was a government effort to put more men to work. The government, however; did not have the money to support the Act. The Act was no more than an idea, but it was probably the most successful program of all times.

Rural homes had no electricity service, so the government encouraged farmers to establish local Co-Ops to purchase electric power from local power generation companies and bring the power lines to the Co-Ops, who in turn would place poles and wire to the farm homes and charge the farmers for the power they used.

My father was a director of a small electric, Co-Op that still exists today, and my brother followed in his footsteps. The day the local power Co-op strapped a cylinder called a transformer to a pole and the switch was pulled to feed the electricity into the house and barn was a happy event.

My father did his wiring, and through the years we found his mistakes, but nothing serious. The common problem was that the material supplied, especially the wire was shabby. Some of the wire was copper covered with tar for insulation and water repellant. Farmers received this poor substitute for the real thing.

Faulty wiring probably caused more fire damage to barns and houses on the farms than all the other causes combined. Consider the huge learning curve for farmers who knew nothing about the power of electricity as they strung wires through their buildings that things weren't much worse.

Barns were my fascination. Every barn had stories to tell of good times, bad times, and sometimes, complaints. Today, Joe Bleighmann's barn screamed, "Help" as I drove past the house to a level spot near the barn entrance.

Joe called to have a vet come out and verify that lightning strike killed his horse. A veterinarian's autopsy that revealed lightning strike meant that Joe received an insurance payment for the worth of the animal.

The crime scene was a sad one. Not only did an old draft horse lay as if it died in agony next to a water tank surrounded by a mud hole, but a heifer also died with the same bulging eyes, tongue hanging out and all four legs extended just like the horse. The young cow's body was still warm. The horse was stone cold.

We didn't have a lightning storm lately. The last storm we had was a week ago when we got dumped on with six inches of snow. Lightning in wintertime does happen occasionally, and if it did, Joe's place would be an excellent destination, so I was cautious about what and how anything was said to this client.

If the report directed the blame on lightening the insurance would promptly pay the farmer. If the diagnosis were something other than lightning in the report to the insurer, the insurance policy would not cover his dead horse.

The autopsy did show a spot of singed hair on the shoulder of the horse, a sign that electrical shock was involved. Joe was in a good mood, probably counting his money from the insurance company. As the scalpel cut through the skin, Joe turned on his threatening voice, and said gruffly, "What are you doing?" I explained that there had to be in my report the description of the tissue under the skin that would give the diagnosis of the lightening strike. Or not.

What I was looking for and not seeing was the telltale red streak of cooked vessels under the skin where the one billion volts of electricity from a lightning bolt hit the spot on the shoulder, then raced toward the ground. There was no evidence of Joe's preference of diagnosis.

The second reason to rule out lightning strike was the presence of the Guernsey heifer that did not die from the same lightning bolt but within minutes before my arrival. The only good news for Joe today was that there would be no reason to charge him for another autopsy because there was another reason for both animals' deaths. The killer was lurking directly over our heads.

An old wire left over from the early days of the Rural Electrification Act thirty years earlier was hanging loosely alongside the barn, apparently not attached to any insulator. It showed the green patina of copper wire visible between shredded insulation.

The power line came in proximity to the steel water pipe that brought the water to the steel water container. The animals were drinking from the container when the electric line came in contact with the steel pipe connected to the tank. The electric shock killed them instantly while they were drinking.

We were in danger. All it would take was a puff of the wind to swing that bare electric line over to touch us where we stood in the mud to kill two stupid men. Include me as one of them; the stupid one who knew better!

Explaining this to Joe was impossible until a breeze came along and slapped the wire against the water pipe causing a "bzzt" sound with sparks. Joe had nothing on his mind at the time beyond having me sign off on the lightning strike and get this dumb vet off his farm.

Joe was sputtering. "Man, I'll show you you're wrong. I'm just going to go over there and put my arm all the way up to my shoulder in that tank, and I'll show you're wrong."

My God! This guy was going to kill himself. He wasn't hearing anything except that he wasn't getting the report signing off lightning strike as the reason for the death of the horse. Out of my frustration, I grabbed a weathered board next to the barn intending to use it as a prop it to keep the wire from touching the water pipe. Immediately it dawned on me how foolish that would be. The old plank pulled out of the manure was soaking wet! If the wire touched the wet wood, I would be the one electrocuted.

What failed in an attempt to keep the moving wire from touching something was now a weapon! The temptation to swing that dirty wet plank alongside Joe's head or anywhere else that would keep him from dipping his arm into the water tank was a strong one, even if it sounded stupid.

Joe stopped in his tracks as the sound of the electric current from the wire found the pipe again, and this time, the noise was close enough to hear clearly. "What would happen if I touched the water?" he asked timidly. I told him that he would die of electrocution. "Just don't do it! If you try to kill yourself, maybe I could resuscitate you, but after I'm gone, nobody's here to help you!"

Suddenly Joe wasn't mad anymore. He was more scared than mad, finally. Joe needed to get educated on things about electricity. First, we turned off the electricity to the barn. Then we put electrical tape around the loose wires and attached the wire to insulators so the wire was nowhere near anything metal or even near the barn because a wet barn carried the electric charge to the ground and could still kill livestock nearby.

Apparently, Joe was already aware something was wrong with his barn's electrical system. Joe's fuse box was a homemade wooden box with the electric line attached to a light socket but without a bulb. Inside the socket instead of a bulb, Joe had jammed pennies into that socket with a hammer and punch. He admitted it was the only way that he could keep his milking machine running.

On my way into town, I stopped at Ken Stoffts place. He did the electrical wiring for the new poultry houses that were going up all over the area. His eyes got big when heard Joe's story.

Ken started to fix Joe's electrical mess, but he didn't finish the job, and he wasn't going to. Ken Stofft never offered why he would not complete the electrical repair, but I can imagine he endured Joe's personality up to a point.

As for my relationship with Joe, he hasn't called in for our services. It is probable that this will be the last we see of Joe until the insurance company pays for his animals that were struck by lightening.

Preventive Medicine for Grunt

Veterinarians find that accident wound repair never has the same condition happening over and over again. Lacerations were the most difficult to guess what we were required to bring to the animal in need. The wounds were often severe and occasionally fatal. On farm animals, the injury was almost always dirty, contaminated, and challenging to treat. Sometime during the treatment, the doctor wondered how to prevent the unfortunate event in the first place.

Treating cows and horses with wounds gave opportunities to work on some big and nasty lacerations. At some point, we got tired of all those "opportunities." It didn't take long before I started to think about how to prevent those kinds of calls.

Something seemed wrong about waiting for a call that an animal was in big trouble. We rushed out to save the animal on an emergency basis. The drama made no sense to me. Some of those calls that came in at all hours of the day and night should not happen. That nobody thought about prevention bothered me.

Opportunities have a way of ambushing a person. We treated a few horses in our Fort Recovery practice, just enough of these noble beasts to keep from getting rusty.

Jerry Switzer owned six big beautiful Clydesdale draft horses that he hauled to shows and pulling contests in five states. One morning, one of his geldings, "Grunt" was down. It looked like he couldn't get up without a lot of help. "Grunt" may rhyme with "Runt," but there was nothing little about this big boy. He weighed more than two thousand pounds of muscle and majesty. To give an idea of how big these Clydesdale horses were, Grunt's foot measured twelve inches across the sole. He was also as gentle as a sweet, trained puppy.

When I arrived, Grunt was standing, but he could not, or would not move his feet. He stood there shivering in pain. His head was down, and his usual soulful eyes were closed. I could not get a look at the bottoms of any foot. Normally it's not a problem to lift a horse's foot. They do it for you.

Both front feet felt hot to the touch, suggesting there were infected abscesses on each front foot. We needed to take a look at the bottoms of those feet. I suggested we use a rope to make him lie down (the term in horse care is "cast"). Jerry beat me to a better solution that saved us an hour of hard work. He "clucked" with his tongue a couple of times and the big horse painfully repositioned himself flat on his side, exposing all four soles.

Looking back at us from the bottom of Grunt's two front feet were three roofing nail heads. Two nails were in the middle of the left sole and one on the outer rim of the sensitive lamina of the right front foot. When I removed them with a pair of pliers, used to remove horseshoe nails, especially the sore right foot, I received a huge, "Thank you" grunt.

Without moving the horse and without using any anesthesia we were able to trim away soft infectious material, allowing drainage of the abscesses that developed over the last few days. A spurt of black smelly juice indicated we were paring away at the correct locations. Then we proceeded to expose the damaged hoof tissue of the abscess. A waterproof bandage with duct tape closed over an antiseptic pad.

After that, a single "Cluck" from his best buddy, Jerry, Grunt got up with his namesake grunt. No longer did his eyes have that sick and sore look. He nudged Jerry's arm. I read that gesture as, "I'm OK now Boss. Do I have to get a shot? Please say no!"

"Grunt" did indeed get a "shot"; he received several in fact. One was a toxoid for tetanus, a common and deadly problem. Always after removing a nail or whatever they manage to get punctured by, tetanus has to be addressed as a danger. If the animal was not treated aggressively for tetanus or as it is more commonly known as "lockjaw", the horse often died a horrible death within three weeks.

The second injection was Penicillin, a lot of it. Although the abscessed area was only as big as one ounce of infected material, we had to treat all 2,000 pounds of the horse once a day for seven days.

We did a walk around the barn and the area that the horses occupied for the last week. A shed that protected the hay from the weather had a roof repair. Two horses, Grunt and Sam, were used to haul the lumber and metal pieces to a landfill on his property within the last week. The grounds produced a dozen roofing nails just like the ones we took from Grunt's feet.

The "walk around" was to find potential trouble conditions for both man and the animals in his care. It struck me that this extra effort felt very rewarding in that we did find several things to fix, and also that this "walk around" was very underused. The seed of an idea was taking life!

A cold shudder crossed my neck and spread down my back. We suddenly had a bigger problem than we realized. By five days, the tetanus bacteria developed its poison, and in two weeks more this horse would be dead because the injection I gave would not protect Grunt until three weeks after the toxoid vaccination. Grunt was not safe; it would be a week too late to help Grunt.

We sent Jerry's wife to our clinic for a bottle of tetanus antitoxin to treat this situation. This tetanus serum gave Grunt immediate protection. At the clinic, we always had six 500 cc bottles of anti-serum when an animal was in danger and had no protection against tetanus. I wouldn't quit until the serum was slowly injected intramuscularly or subcutaneously (IM or SQ). The debris and tissue we trimmed from Grunt's feet and the contaminated ground were collected to take back to the clinic for incineration.

Next, we looked at Sam's feet, the other horse on the work detail with exposure to the roofing nails. We had to make sure he didn't have the same problem as Grunt. When we checked Sam, all four feet were good – no sign of any injury to the soles or the skin.

I then vaccinated all the horses with the toxoid that protected them from tetanus within a few days if they were up to date with their yearly vaccinations. Vaccinations once every two years would be sufficient if there was no history of tetanus on the premise, but that was not the case here because Jerry's farm had a history of sheep dying from tetanus. Jerry didn't know for sure if his vaccine for the horses included tetanus, saying, "Let me check on that."

We went to his refrigerator to see what Jerry's tetanus prevention protocol revealed. We discovered he had none for the last six years. The horses had everything but tetanus. I was astounded.

Jerry gave his horses their "shots" faithfully every year, so he thought that included everything. As a veterinarian, the combination vaccine included tetanus in every equine vaccine. I didn't even know the vaccine Jerry used was available.

The penalty for a veterinarian to mistakenly leave tetanus out of the vaccination process was at least censure or as drastic as losing the license to practice. Jerry bought his vaccines at a tractor supply store. He was not aware that all his horses were in danger. Jerry was one lucky horse owner. In the case of all six animals, we scheduled a "booster" vaccination of tetanus toxoid in six weeks, including Grunt, and yearly vaccinations with the toxoid.

Tetanus is a terrible disease caused by a bacterium, Clostridium tetanii, and all warm-blooded animals, including man, are susceptible to tetanus. The bacterium can morph into a spore when its' environment becomes intolerable and would otherwise kill most bacteria.

Those spores lived a long time in the soil. In our classes on equine diseases, we understood that we should think that the spores live forever once they are in the dirt. Forever was at least three thousand years.

If an animal like a horse died from tetanus, how many bacteria do you suppose were involved in the horse's death? The answer is a few hundred thousand. How many of those bacteria will survive as a life form called a spore? The answer is every last one of them!

The spores change back to viable bacteria with a favorable environment in deep wounds with the absence of oxygen. Soon it divided and became two bacteria, and those two became four until an abscess formed with millions, even billions of bacterial cells. Those cells make the toxin that affects the nervous system.

Continuing on our walk around the farm, looking for nails, in particular, I noted things that could cause problems. An old rusted railroad spike pounded into a beam in the barn a long time ago was our first find. It was crooked, leaving several inches exposed and it was at about the right height off the ground where it could rip into the side of any one of those big horses running into the barn. A wound of that dimension required at least a hundred stitches to repair. Jerry fixed that accident waiting to happen, in short order, with a crowbar and a sledgehammer.

Concerning the cleanup around the roof repair, I suggested for him to go to a hardware store and buy a magnet designed to find and pick up nails in the dirt. I would bet there were a lot more nails we missed.

Also, a mud hole in the yard seemed to be the favorite place for the horses to hang out. Jerry explained that the water line to the barn had a leak causing the wet spot. He didn't think it was important. After all, the soft mud became the horses' favorite meeting place. Asked if he knew what "thrush" in horses had in common with mud holes; he knew, and he was getting the message.

The serum was ready to inject IM and SQ, so for the next twenty minutes, Jerry became quite talkative. We were talking about our preventive medicine programs for dairies, and Jerry asked, "Why don't you do something like you just did for me and call it preventive medicine?"

That was when I told myself that Jerry just gave me validation of the feeling earlier that as a veterinarian preaching preventative medicine, I should include a lot more "walk-around" sessions in my farm calls.

SERENDIPITY

"Something strange is happening here", I said, talking out loud to myself after looking through the binoculars of the microscope for at least the tenth time. A fresh glass slide with a small drop of intestinal cell scraping was pressed under a cover slip. It was shimmering in the muted light source.

This was the third time witnessing this strange phenomenon. There had to be an important key missing. All three cases involved the same house of young turkeys over a span of three weeks. The prime suspect had to be a life form to be the cause of this flock being sick rather than a nutritional excess or deficiency. Whatever caused the shimmering had to be something living in there, under the microscope as we were observing it.

Beau, the field technician for Olding Mills Turkey Farms brought the latest samples of birds for autopsy. The flock was generally unthrifty for a month, and by this time Beau was reporting a rising mortality. The birds were from the morning's mortality group, meaning they just died.

The signs all indicated a parasitic infestation by a protozoan disease called coccidiosis. Conventional treatments with Amprolium and sulfas in the water were not effective. Three laboratories, including ours found no evidence of coccidiosis or worm infestation.

The statement came to mind, "What the mind cannot perceive, the eyes will not believe." That statement was the key to understand the unknown. There was no profession that witnessed strange things more frequently than a veterinarian. By the way, that statement above belongs to the Greek philosopher Plato, 2400 years ago.

My microscope was a good quality Leitz binocular instrument that had the capability of magnifying the field of study up to 1200 times under immersion oil preparation. Up to now, the 480 X magnification optic was believed to be powerful enough to identify any parasite known.

Maybe it was time to test that standard. The only thing that was consistent so far was a strange shimmering, like something moving the material trapped between the glass slides.

What made tissue move and shimmer? The chase was narrowing down to just a few possibilities. The search was for something small and something that refracted light, or bent light, like a prism. Some possibilities considered were protozooae, small worms; tiny enough to be transparent, and some other small but active lower life forms.

All the equipment and stains needed were on the table, ready to finally solve the puzzle. This was exciting stuff until you considered what the excitement was all about.

One more idea; I placed a small drop of raw intestinal columnar cells on a glass slide and mixed a larger drop of immersion oil into it, and then lowered the 1200 times magnification optic into the drop.

What appeared very clearly identified the "shimmer" agent. Worms! Very tiny worms were moving. The shimmer effect was the bending of light that passed through the moving transparent parasites that were still alive.

That tiny drop of tissue contained about two thousand live worms. To get an idea of how small those worms were, an erythrocyte (red blood cell) covered three worms end to end. A red blood cell in birds is about ten microns in diameter so the worms were three microns in length and its' width about five percent of its' length. By adjusting the light, it showed that about half the worms carried, and were releasing tiny transparent eggs.

Beau and I had a Jaycee meeting of officers scheduled at six, so we adjourned to the back table at Thobe's Restaurant and continued the topic of discovery of a new worm for a while. Not one of the Jaycees' officers thought the worm thing was a big deal. Robbie Fleischmeister suggested, "Whatever you do, please don't name the little critter after your wife! Ho, ho, ho."

The later classification identified that it was a new worm never before reported. It was related to the hookworm, of which there were thousands of varieties. In general, they were a nasty parasite, living off their host's blood.

The parasite treatment available commercially was piperazine, a product introduced into the water of the turkeys.

According to a salesperson of the manufacturer, "Piperazine puts the worm to sleep and when the worm wakes up, the host (the turkey) is gone." Well, in any case, the treatment had no effect on the parasite load of the birds in the flock we were treating.

Purdue University suggested that a plant growing in Central America called Leucaena leucophala might be helpful. It was used effectively as a folk medicine for larger forms of the hookworm species.

In one of our brainstorming sessions with the owner of Olding Mills, field techs from St Clair Mills and Beau, we thought our best work would be to interrupt the life cycle of the parasite. Beau suggested that since only one house with 5,000 turkeys were involved and the parasite's effects were more in the category of a nuisance, the worm might be a recent mutant and not very strong.

If that were the case, it should be easy to break its life cycle. Probably no more than a hundred birds died so far. The thought was worthy of testing so we brought out our old college textbooks on parasite life cycles and how to break the cycle. There were over a hundred and fifty different life cycles to study.

The plan of attack was agreed upon and was put into action the next day. The two month-old birds ere moved to a new facility they were working on. The new house did not allow the droppings to accumulate where the turkeys could peck at the feces and re-introduce the worm eggs back into the bird's gut, thus interrupting the life cycle of the parasite.

The old turkey barn was burned to the ground and anything left was incinerated in our clinic crematory. That was another method of interrupting the life cycle, especially if wild birds or foot traffic played a role in its spread.

The plan worked. The small flock performed about average and the mortality was stopped. When they left the new house, the feces under the screen floor was collected and cremated. Then the building was sanitized and left empty for two years. No further cases occurred.

The young men in the Jaycees had it right. It was no big deal that I discovered a new worm and named it after myself. The name, Cooperia

<u>cooperia var. tebbensesis</u> became obscure, then changed during the peer review by scientists who spent their life studying parasites.

Taxonomy is the system known as Linnaean classification for categorization of organisms and binomial nomenclature for naming organisms. There really are scientists who spend their time classifying the hookworm family. This is a very large family of more than two hundred thousand distinctly different species, sub-species, etc.

The parasite I discovered was named after me. I felt slighted at first when the taxonomist changed the name, but after studying deeper, I found they classified the tiny species by the length of the male worm's cuticular pedicle.

It doesn't matter if the correct scientific name for the penis of a worm is called a cuticular pedicle, but you get the idea. My little worm had the world's smallest penis. Now he is named after someone else, thank God!

If that taxonomist ever calls me to take naming rights of that worm back, the answer will be, "No!"

BLACK MACK

Mule stories are my favorites. I don't know what God thought when He created the mule; in fact, there's evidence that God had nothing to do with it at all. God created the horse and the donkey. I suspect a little burro with a big sex drive couldn't help himself when he saw that sexy fat rump of a particular mare, flagging her tail. Helping himself he did, and probably the lady horse as well. And that is where mules originated. And God said, "Thou shall not procreate." The mules have been sterile ever since, but they figured out a way to get around that edict.

Mules are smarter than any horse, most people, but not a dog. They are strong, sure-footed, and are aware of everything happening around them. Once I watched a mule Jenny study the farrier in her pen. Slowly she maneuvered the man into a corner, but she meant no harm to the farrier — just to scare him. I chose to intervene by climbing into the pen and distract the animal. It came to me in an instant that she was not after the farrier; she intentionally lured me into the pen.

Instantly she jumped into the air and turned a 270-degree circle and parked her butt directly facing me. I made it out of the pen between the ground and the first bar. Once I stood upright on the outside, she struck the bars with both back feet, and then stood there like nothing happened.

I am sure the Jenny had no intention of hurting anybody. She was just playing! You could see it in her eyes! She also had a big smile on those big lips of hers!

The story of "Black Mack" started when I visited a friend I worked with in southern Ohio as an artificial breeding technician. Charles applied for and secured the job as the new dairy herd manager at one of the state prison farms.

The huge yard at the prison was as neat as a park. One prison inmate called a "trusty" had the job of driving the biggest animal I've ever seen up close. "Black Mack" was old then, but for his age, he was majestic! I stand a little less than six feet tall, and the mule's shoulders were a good foot above my head. He was the only horse or mule I've ever seen that measured over twenty hands high.

His duties were not so difficult; he pulled a cart about twice as big as a wheelbarrow for the trusty who picked up trash. The mule was officially too old to be working according to the prison's directives.

Charles was still the herdsman for the penitentiary three years into my veterinary practice in Fort Recovery. The prison was only about sixty miles from Fort Recovery. He called to find out if I could help him with a problem at the penitentiary farm. "Black Mack" was now more than forty years old. He was thin and wasn't eating. It was long past time to put him to sleep.

Charles' problem was that no veterinarian would do it. It was easy for me to accept his plea to come over and give 'black Mack" an injection that would put the mule to sleep, then deeper until he died painlessly. It would also be good to catch up with my old friend.

I arrived two days later; three trustys held the big black mule in the big yard. Each man was hanging on to his rope attached to an old custom made halter just for Black Mack. Charles told me that the mule practically had to be dragged to move.

The big black mule I remembered was a majestic animal that stood twenty hands high. That was twelve years since I last saw him. On this visit, he was in bad shape with his ribs so prominent on his chest and his bones pressing against his matted hair. I felt so sad because of what he used to be.

One 500 cc bottle was enough to euthanize any horse. I brought two. The men held the halter ropes as I introduced the needle into the jugular vein. Mack didn't move, so he received both bottles. His head dropped lower and lower until his nose touched the ground. He was sleeping standing up.

My injection wasn't working! The prison orders were that weapons were not allowed on the farm except for the guards, so a bullet wasn't an option. As a last resort to finish this job I took a bottle of an older formula of euthanasia solution in my bag to inject into the jugular vein quickly.

The first reaction was a deep breath, and then the mule shook himself and reared up! Black Jack jerked all three men holding their ropes off their feet. This animal was so tall that one of the men was five feet off the ground. As one man let go of the rope, he fell on his back. As Black Jack's feet came down, one foot landed directly on his chest!

I was in the middle of this melee. The mule was moving now, slow and deliberately. Two of the men were still holding on to the halter. I started to care for the injured man and called to the men on the ropes to release his harness and let Mack go. I needed help to get the wounded man to the infirmary.

A glance at Mack gave me a glimpse of the mule slowly pushing against a fence with a cornfield on the other side. The fence was a "Hog Fence," five feet tall with fence posts every eight feet. Those posts were popping out of the ground as Mack slowly and powerfully kept pushing until the fence was flat on the ground. Mack aimlessly walked over a knoll and disappeared in the cornfield.

We gently placed the injured inmate in the bed of Charles' truck for the short ride to the infirmary. He was under oxygen pressure for his crushed lungs within seconds once at the infirmary. It seemed like an eternity. A medic helicopter soon landed to take the injured man to the University Hospital in nearby Columbus.

The helpers and Charles gathered to talk about what just happened. Charles had to explain a lot to the warden.

The first dose, although a massive amount, was not enough to continue depressing Black Mack to the point where he would die. The second medication had a different activity in the mule's brain and heart. It acted as an antidote to the first injection. It woke him up, big time! He wasn't going to die, but my guess was that we did damage to parts of his brain that would likely affect his behavior. There was a strong possibility he would become aggressive, or at least unpredictable.

Reports from Charles and the warden indicated the injured man was recovering slowly and that he wanted to relay his thanks to the vet for saving his life. That helped me because I felt that I was to blame his injuries.

The mule was eating a hole in the cornfield, and he certainly did show aggression from the first, so they left him alone in the field. It was time for me to return and finish the task.

Six weeks after the failed attempt to put Mack to sleep, I returned to the prison. Charles met me with, "The Old Man wants to see you." (The Old Man was the warden.) We entered the director's office to find him sitting behind his big desk with a WWI Springfield rifle in his hands. "I figured you would want to finish this job yourself, he said. You will have three armed guards to back you up. Just in case."

We discussed the mule's behavior the last couple of weeks. "Black Mack is so old that he is unpredictable. He has become a danger, said the warden. There's a half-acre of the cornfield that is completely bare because Mack compulsively attacks anything in his space, including weeds. If anyone steps into the open arena, Mack will charge, but when he gets to the standing corn, he will not go into it."

Charles added, "I took a bucket of water for him, and he charged me. When I stepped just a little way into the corn, Mack stopped, turned and walked away. I guess he gets his water needs from the growing corn and the developing ears that by now were big roasting ear size."

The warden handed me the Springfield rifle and said, "There is one round to get the job done. You get only one chance. My men will save you if it's necessary." For a moment I thought John Wayne was talking to me at the Alamo. The warden even sounded like John Wayne!

The field changed since the corn stalks were a foot high when we watched Mack tear down a hundred feet of fencing. We walked several hundred yards or more through corn plants easily ten feet high to get to where Black Mack was standing at the opposite end of a clearing.

He was not skinny anymore. It was evident that he was able to hear and had decent sight. I slipped a single round into the breech, and the safety was off. I stepped into the bare patch in the cornfield and shouted to the mule. Black Mack sorted out where the noise was coming from; standing stock still at first, then he trotted stiffly, slowly picking up speed. He now thundered toward me. It didn't seem terribly intense, and I didn't feel threatened. The tall corn would be there to hide me if necessary. As he got into the range where I couldn't miss at twenty yards, I pulled the trigger, and the round hit him between the eyes and a bit higher. A perfect shot.

Mack kept coming. It wasn't a charge, but I expected him to drop like a stone. I started to back up so the guards could get a clear shot when Mack stumbled and finally crumpled at my feet.

Now it was evident why nobody wanted to do the execution. There was no reason for me to feel good.

Charles told me years ago that Black Mack was the only friend for so many men in that prison. The mule performed as a psychotherapist for hundreds of inmates over the years, as he listened to their stories why they shouldn't be in jail.

The warden decided to make this event with Mack a special occasion. He allowed any of the inmates who wished to say goodbye to Mack, one at a time to pay their last respects.

One inmate who was in this prison longer than anyone could remember told us that he watched the long-legged foal being born in a stall on a rainy Fourth of July morning, forty-three years ago!

Bloat

A cow is a ruminant and has four stomachs instead of only one. People, dogs and a lot of animals have one stomach. The horse manages very well with a single stomach, but in some respects, it digests hay somewhat like a cow does. The digestive process in animals is a complex study in biochemistry, nutrition, fermentation, and changes in the weather.

I struggled through three courses of advanced biochemistry in vet school, and to this day I have to admit that understanding the biochemistry of ruminants didn't come without a struggle.

In Ohio, farmers turned out cows to graze on pastures of grass, protein-rich legumes like clover and alfalfa, and sometimes cornfields after harvest. Good pasturages provided nutritious protein and energy food as it came up from the soil. Early spring pastures of grass and legumes alone delivered a significant boost in milk production.

A metabolic wreck called "bloat" often happened after an overnight rain on a clover or new grass pasture. The cows often ate too much, too fast of the very wet meadow grass and clover. The thin flexible stems of the plants ingested became a tangled mass in the rumen, the second and by far the largest stomach of the four.

Fermentation of the stuff she just gobbled down took place almost immediately. Fermentation made bubbles, and then the bubbles united to form a stinky gas cloud while the stems became twisted like a rope. That twisted mass blocked the escape of gas and liquids passage on down the gut. At that point, we had what is called a "bloated" animal that only had a fifty percent chance of survival without help.

Once a client told me the key to good health was to, "Keep all holes open" That's where the vet comes in. The tools the veterinarian used were the same tools used for two thousand years, maybe longer.

My tools were my speculum, a rigid tube inserted into the mouth, past the tongue, and a long rubber stomach tube passed through the speculum, down the esophagus, and into the cow's second stomach. The third instrument was a trochar; something like an injection needle, but way bigger.

Usually, there was time to place the speculum in the mouth and immediately insert the hose into the rumen. With luck, we got a rush of air relieved from that cloud of trapped gas in the rumen. That was always a good show as twenty to thirty cubic yards of very smelly; combustible gas discharged in ten seconds. That relieved the bloated cow in a relatively short time.

Sometimes we were early in the process when the gas bubbles were still clinging together like foam. In that case, a gallon of mineral oil was pumped into the rumen, releasing surface tension of the foam. That related to the "all holes open" rule.

All too often the cow was dead on our arrival or seconds from death when we got there. If there was simply not enough time to wrestle with a cow about to die, out came the trochar. At a spot on the left side of the cow that was visibly distended more than any place else, I would slam the trochar to the hilt without hesitation, and apply pressure while the gas escaped. There was so much pressure with the escaping gas that someone had to press the trochar hard or it would blow out.

It usually took twenty minutes to bleed off all the gas. If the vet is a showman, he lit the gas coming out the large needle. A flame about ten feet long shot a streak of nearly invisible blue light from the methane released in the gas mix. I wasn't a showman that day — I didn't have a match, darn it!

My brother-in-law Bill was strictly city raised and awestruck at the lifestyle I so happily and enthusiastically lived. Bill was eager to go with me on calls on his visits to Fort Recovery.

On a Sunday morning during breakfast, I received a call from Ed Ebens to treat one of his cows with bloat. Bill, my brother-in-law from Cincinnati, asked if he could come along. I waited for him to say that because I guaranteed him an experience he never forgot. I gave him no warning about what to expect on purpose. "What is bloat?" he asked. "There's no time to explain, so let's roll," I said. Bill scooped up half an omelet to eat along the way.

The cow supposedly was in a back pasture. I had to look for Ed's white pickup truck along the road, which I found okay. The lane was muddy from the last night's shower, and dew collected on leaves and fence lines along the way. The unfortunate cow was in bad shape. Unable to get up, the cow looked like a blimp with all four legs straight out like toothpicks.

The cow was dying and probably had only two or three good breaths left in her. She was lying on the side that I had to strike with my trochar. In an instant I flipped her over, surprised at how little effort it took.

Now the cow was in a better position, so I pushed the trochar into the hilt, releasing a stream of gas and foamy rumen fluid. In the process of pushing the trochar hard, it was impossible to escape from getting splattered by some of the nastiest smelling stuff nature ever provided.

Ed, the owner, never saw this kind of emergency treatment for bloat, so it was no surprise that he became a little belligerent. He sputtered, "Are you crazy? You're killing my cow!"

Ordinarily, we never flip a cow over on her back because there are organs that can become twisted, but with this cow, there was so much pressure that nothing inside was going to move, besides we could never turn her over the other direction with her legs locked like table legs. Time expired for wasted seconds on the old girl.

My audience by now was cautiously watching from twenty feet away. The spray of foul-smelling rumen ingesta must have reached Bill because his breakfast was on the ground. His skin color was somewhere between green and gray. At that moment, Bill was in worse shape than the cow.

Ed felt better about my rough handling of his cow, now that she was able to sit up usually with her feet under her. The pressure seemed to be gone. I had Ed put a halter on the cow to help keep her head raised. I pulled the trochar out and applied pressure on the spot where it had penetrated into the rumen. I needed five minutes of pressure to assure there would be no leakage that might result in infection. Suddenly the cow got up, and Ed went down, holding the halter that slipped off the cow while he was struggling to get it to fit her head. The rest of the herd went to the barn earlier, and in a few more minutes our cow joined them. We were unable to catch her for further treatment.

The cow did fine. Ed told me later, "Well I'll be damned. Good work, Doc."

Bill was in a different mood. He felt sick, and he smelled bad, but not as bad as I did. Anyway, Bill would not ride home with me in the truck. He felt like he would be better off walking the ten miles back to the house. I did smell bad and was also beginning to feel bad that I allowed Bill to get close enough to experience one of the worst practical jokes of farm life ever.

The vet truck saved the day. I had my vet truck for a year. It had almost everything just this kind of emergency. The pickup bed was a customized clinic on wheels. In this case for Bill, he needed a shower and clean coveralls. Bill took a nice warm three-gallon shower next to the truck and changed clothes, so he felt better, but not great.

There was no water, hot or cold left for me. Now Bill still had to decide if he would ride home with his stinky brother-in-law or walk the ten miles. He was OK with my stripping and climbing into a clean coverall, but I had to promise to drive with the windows down.

We climbed into the truck, and suddenly Bill stopped. "How did you do that?" "Do what," I answered. "You don't stink!" he said. I played around with him for a little and finally told him that I used something I learned from him five years earlier.

Bill was a chemist at Proctor & Gamble, the company that makes Crest toothpaste. I used a half tube of his Crest toothpaste in the water bucket that I used to clean my boots. A cold and quick sponge bath before jumping into my coveralls didn't make me clean, but I smelled like mint.

Bill once told me that Crest toothpaste, and probably all the other brands as well contained seven of the most powerful deodorants in the world. Since then I have been using his concoction of two ounces of toothpaste in a gallon of warm water. It made a great body rinse after a long and usually dirty day in the barns.

Bill often rode with me on calls, but I noticed he asked a lot of questions about what was going to happen on the farm visits.

It's all about having the Biggest Tractor

Luke Lamm and his wife were hard workers, even as farmers go. They lived off the highway on the way to Saint Henry, the nearest town to Fort Recovery. The long lane to the farm buildings curved around a copse of young oak trees both beautiful and serviceable as a windbreaker, so it's a good guess that the squirrels didn't plant them as lost acorns. Their house was a two-story brick block structure dating to the Civil War era. It had lots of rooms for a big family.

The outbuildings were less than unremarkable except for an addition to the barn to accommodate a relatively large dairy herd built a dozen years ago. Most of the dairy herds we serviced averaged thirty milking cows. Luke milked from seventy-five to ninety cows, so he was one of the largest dairies in our practice.

The lane was simple but aesthetic in the way it presented the farm and partially hid the farm buildings. The fact that Luke graded that driveway every week with his tractor pulling a real road grader like the county used for the hundreds of miles of our gravel roads sent a message. The lane was the statement of a proud man.

He was justifiably proud of his large family as well. I understood the pride, growing up in a large family of eight myself. Four of my brothers and sisters had eight or more kids. They made family pride understandable.

Luke had the biggest dairy herd, and his machinery was in good shape. His pride and joy was his new tractor that was big enough to handle the tasks for a thousand acre farm.

Luke's farm was only ninety acres and the new tractor cost more than his farm. Either he was a sucker for the implement salesmen or he had a bigger problem. He wasn't paying anything on his invoices we sent for over a year and his business with us had been trailing off to nothing.

Gretta called on the new two-way radio we were trying out before buying. It wasn't working very well, and we already determined the radio was going back. Her message was "scratchy, " and all that came through was, "Luke" and "Henry" or was it "hurry"?

Since there were three Lukes in the vicinity of Saint Henry, it would be a slim chance it would be Luke Lamm. Guessed wrong again.

Our communications between the office and the ambulatory vehicles were beyond unsatisfactory. We needed something like a telephone in our pocket, but until some fantastic comes along, we will have to be satisfied with what little common sense we have.

Eventually, Luke Lamm's pretty lane that I admired so much came into view.

As soon as the vet truck stopped, six kids took off running with the message that Doc Tebbe was here to see "Daddy." It was interesting that after six boys and girls had run off, there were still three kids left, staring at me and saying nothing. I recognized one of them, Leo, and after three stuttering tries, he said, "Hi Doc," so we finally got some communication. He told me that he didn't know what Daddy wanted, but his daddy was pretty mad.

I heard Luke's tractor long before it came around the barn. The three smaller children rode with him in the cab of the tractor, and the other three barefooted kids were making little clouds of dust of their own.

There was no sign that Luke was angry about anything. He seemed to be glad to see me. In fact, the first thing he said was, "Doc, I'm happy you came."

"Doc, I want you to show me how to make my cows produce more milk than my neighbor, Tom Stein," he announced straightforwardly.

That was a big order since Tom's Holstein dairy herd was one of the best-managed dairies in the county, and Tom, who was a leading dairyman for years was also using all our new programs' resources for about two years.

Our practice offered dairy health planning meetings twice a month at the new clinic location that used to be a beer joint. Food and drinks maybe were the reason we had a great response from the dairymen. Luke was at several of these meetings lately.

We often had an outside speaker who was able to teach the veterinarians as well. The topic the night Luke last attended was about dairy herd nutrition, and we presented how to gather feed samples for analysis, how to mix the farm's hay, silage and homegrown corn and oats with specific supplements to balance what the cows ate perfectly.

Calories fed to cows were measured carefully and in balance with other nutrients. It was not uncommon for a high producing cow to consume well over a hundred thousand calories a day. In return, those cows produced twelve or more gallons of milk in a day, and they were able to keep up this level of production for months.

Tom Stein had several super cows producing up to one hundred pounds of milk a day and so did more than a few other dairymen. Herds like Tom's had ten generations of superior genetics specifically chosen to increase milk and butterfat production, but they still benefitted in terms of fewer sick cows with healthy diets. Luke had no super cows, but those he had could perform a lot better with our help.

Everybody was amazed at the things we were able to do with computers and the promise of the future impact on the dairy industry due to computer use.

Well, I have to admit that I was pretty excited too. Computers in 1966 were big hot machines that processed individual punch cards representing one cow at a time. With magic, a large printer spits out a long, wide sheet of information and detailed recommendations of feeding. Evidentially Luke was impressed too.

"How much is that going to cost?" he tentatively asked, since we had been talking about the nutrition program for a while. I gave Luke an approximate figure for a herd his size. "No. I want the whole shebang. The way it is now, the cows are barely making a profit".

Well, I would have to agree with that. Luke's managing this herd so far was a disaster. Our program was not all about nutrition that he needed. Our team could help him with financial records, care for those cows preparing to have their calves within two months (the "dry" cows), reproduction, and pregnancy checkups.

Other professionals on our team were the milking machine equipment salespeople and artificial insemination technicians. Luke needed to use the skills these two businesses represented. The milking machine representative could fix Luke's vacuum system, and within a week, solve the problem of mastitis (sore udders, infected milk, and less milk to sell). The insemination technician had a different challenge. His job was to teach the dairyman how important it was to use genetic selection to transform the next generations' ability to produce more milk, more efficiently. If Luke wanted to be like Tom Stein, these two businesses had to help in Luke's dairy management.

Luke was crestfallen, but he wasn't a quitter when it came to bartering. "Can't we work it out where I pay with the extra profits?" It was evident Luke had been thinking about the herd health program and put in some quality thinking time in what he wanted to accomplish overall. He saw this as the answer for everything.

What Luke wanted was to make three times more profit from his cows than he did last year. That was reasonable. His profit from last year's records was not enough to support his family, without any mention of what that new tractor was costing him on monthly payments.

He wanted a lifeline, and I was just as desperate to give him one for the sake of his family. He also didn't want to pay the vet clinic anything unless and until we got his profit level up. If it didn't work, he would pay us nothing. Luke's proposal was, if our program did succeed, then he would pay our veterinary clinic five percent of the extra profit.

"What do you think, Doc?" I considered that his "test the water" figure wouldn't fly, but I didn't say it. The man had his bargaining face on, so I worked on the percentage and got him up to twenty percent of profit per cow more than $450. According to last year's records, he made a small profit of $150 per cow.

After doing a thorough analysis of his herd, the nutrition challenge revealed a seriously out of balance between phosphorous and calcium. This imbalance was partly the reason for his history of treating paralyzed cows.

Why didn't we as veterinarians see what was causing his paralyzed cows? The simple reason is that Luke didn't want help from vets that knew less than he did. He used four different vet clinics and rarely sent them a payment for services. None of the veterinarians considered Luke a model client.

Things had to be very grave for Luke to swallow his pride and ask for help. After seeing those nine children, all under thirteen years old, I felt honored Luke invited me to help him; rather, help his family. Luke was a jerk, but there was hope.

The cows were eating dirt for years. There was a huge hole in a permanent pasture behind the barn. It was deep enough to hide twenty cows standing up. Luke had never mentioned that his cows were eating their way to China.

Over the years the imbalance of calcium and phosphorus alone was responsible for many cases of milk fever and an unacceptable low fertility record in Luke's herd. Also, Luke did not feed much grain, especially corn, which was high in energy and essential amino acids (protein). He was selling his corn from his farm because it gave him cash. He liked cash!

The balanced ration being fed in adequate amounts to support higher production gave us the first visible results. Within three months we were halfway to the payday goal.

Spangler's Milking Machine Service did a complete job evaluating the system and fixing the problems without a huge cost. All they had to do was to provide the correct amount of vacuum pressure and replace the pain causing cups. Immediately his mastitis problem vanished, and the cows were easier to handle at milking time.

The cows were fed an amount of grain in the milking parlor according to the pounds of milk they produced. By October or about four months or less, the profit average per cow was over $500 on a yearly basis. Luke was making a lot of money now and even seemed OK that the vet was going to get some of it. We kept working on the project because there was still a lot to be done.

Getting Luke's cows pregnant on time so they had a calf approximately once a year was necessary for high milk production. When a cow gave birth to a calf, it stimulated the production of milk. Luke's had cows that produced an enormous amount of milk, but not enough. Most of the unproductive cows were related to "Old Charley," a beef cow, not noted for having daughters that give milk.

When we started our fertility program for Luke, we put a lot of emphasis on selecting particular bulls by using artificial insemination that would increase the chances of having increased production for the next generations. That part of the program failed miserably.

The first good sign was when "Old Charley", Luke's old crossbreed bull lost interest in his fatherly chore and had to go somewhere else. Throughout his rule in the yard, Old Charley was the only animal, including humans that knew when a cow was in heat and when to breed them.

Luke was too busy to spend the time watching his cows for signs of estrus. He didn't have a chance to call the technician to come out to service the cow. The solution was to train one or more of the children to watch the cows twice a day.

Finally and reluctantly, Susan, a fifteen-year-old freckled redhead took over that chore and by the end of the year she had the artificial insemination part on the track. With our help, Susan gave every cow in the herd their handpicked "BIAS" (Boyfriend in a Straw) for artificial insemination.

With this program of genetic selection, the superior genetics expected from this program would take place three years in the future. The only way finally I got the idea into Luke's head was to tell him he will never beat Tom's production until his herd genetics were as good as that of Tom's herd.

At the end of the first full year of profit above goal, Luke had realized his goal and then some, and so did our veterinary center. His check for almost nine thousand dollars made him the second best client in our practice after the giant turkey and chicken account.

Although Luke begrudged paying the vets so much, he had to be happy that we increased his profits seven and one-half times over the previous year. Want to guess what he spent with his earnings? Would you even think of trading a perfectly good two-year-old tractor in on a newer and bigger tractor?

The second year was also dependent on being paid twenty percent over the profit from the year just finished. We advised Luke to cull some cows and replace a few with new additions from Tom Stein's herd, thus reducing Luke's number of cows milked from ninety cows average to seventy-six in the second year. His net income with fewer cows increased his profit by thirty percent.

He paid us less than half, which came in sporadic installments through the year. He informed us that he would not be renewing a contract for another year because it made his vet bill too high. He even complained that he had to buy a much bigger stainless steel milk tank to hold the extra milk the cows produced.

Luke's math reasoning was a bit convoluted. He didn't want to pay the veterinary clinic anything. When I told him that the difference of the money in his pocket the second year was enough to pay off his tractor, he became quiet.

After Luke had dropped out of our program, our infrequent calls to Luke's farm revealed nutritional problems and lower production but not as dangerously low as when we started, but Luke had lost interest in the cows.

Another veterinarian, Dr. Chalmers was also making calls to the farm. Dr. Chalmers, a new graduate of Purdue University, stopped at our clinic to introduce himself and to discuss how he could follow up with what we started with Luke. We talked a lot about herd health programs and the veterinarian's role as a manager. He accepted our invitation to join us in presenting some of the classes.

My advice to Dr. Chalmers was to give Luke his best effort, but don't let him charge it on his account. That may be my sage advice to Dr. Chalmers but the advice I had a serious problem applying it to myself.

The two years managing Luke's herd was quite a challenge, and believe me; there were lots of eyes on the outcome from the dairy community. The very positive public relations value of taking a problem herd to a successful one in two years might be what Luke meant when he thought he didn't owe us anything.

Luke's daughter Susan had been coming to the meetings since she was in high school and even conducted an evening presentation on sire selection for credit on public speaking for her FFA project (Future Farmers of America).

She expressed concerns for her father, "He no longer had any interest in anything but crop farming and he recently bought a larger farm in Indiana, eighteen miles away from home."

Susan talked to me about becoming a doctor, but her family would not be able to afford to send her to college. Susan met four girls who were our babysitters, all four already in colleges or aimed in that direction. Their families could not afford college for their girls, but they received scholarships all the way to their doctorates.

The girls kind of adopted Susan as a sister and guided her in the direction of her choice. If there ever was a happy ending to a story, this relationship of five farm girls all made it as doctors of sorts.

Soon it was almost a daily occurrence in Fort Recovery to see Luke driving a bigger tractor than the last one through town, smoking a big cigar, and leading a parade of one with a big smile on his face and waving to people on the sidewalks.

The end came soon enough. Luke had to make a choice to keep the tractor and his new farm or keep his home farm that had been in the family since 1870 and get serious about being a dairyman.

His choice was to sell the dairy. Selling the farm was a good economic move for Luke and for the young farmer who bought the old farm with the lovely lane, the old house, and a herd of cows that were ready to respond to someone who cared.

Luke did what was best for him. The money from selling the home place and the dairy helped him negotiate purchasing another Indiana farm. He then had more than the thousand acres needed to justify his big tractors. Soon enough he became my best customer again. This time it was the corn and soybeans he sold off the farm for cash. My newly acquired Busy Bee Mills bought and sold his entire crop. Of course, I had to negotiate a good deal for him.

He was a happy man again and his family adapted well in the rolling hills of Indiana. I am sure his family made an impression on the Jay County school system for years to come if the other ten kids followed their big sister Susan's example

Fred Woodson moves to Mississippi

When I was a kid growing up on a farm ten miles north of Fort Recovery, the wooded hills around the town held a fascination for me from the time I could ride a bike the distance.

My school library had few books, but someone from the Fort Recovery Historical Society kept an entire bookshelf in all the surrounding elementary schools filled with accounts of the Indian battles after the Revolutionary War.

The maps located the camp of Chief Little Turtle's army of 2,000 warriors. It was surprisingly close to where Chief Little Turtle ambushed the United States Army. The result of that battle gave it the distinction of being the worst defeat of any American Army battle to this day.

The Indian war party camped on what in 1962 was Fred Woodson's farm on the spot along the Wabash River at the base of several hills less than a mile from the scene of the battle. My friends and I collected buckets of arrowheads, spear points and lots of Tomahawk stones from the old camping grounds of Little Turtle.

Two other items held my interest. First, there was a pond on the farm that never froze over, and it had a lot of catfish, and second, there were interesting (and pretty) girls living at the farm, but I was too bashful to say, "Hi."

Returning to my hometown fifteen years later, one of my first excursions was to the Woodson farm. Fred's dad had died, and Fred took over the family farm. The old catfish hole was still there. It struck me as interesting how little those catfish were. Fred assured me they were always "little buggers."

Fred loved to farm. It seemed that maybe it was work that he loved. Fred was a hard worker and spent long hours caring for a sizeable dairy herd, lots of chickens, and pigs. He made a good living from the farm, but he didn't count his compensation as dollars; rather the opportunity to work long and hard hours, get a little sleep and start all over the next day.

About six years later Fred caught up with me in Haywood's Hardware store and invited me to come to his farm to "'Show something to you." I was curious and had an hour to kill so I followed Fred to the farm.

He told me, "I'm going to sell the farm with all the livestock and machinery and put the money in a suitcase and move to Mississippi." "Does anybody know about this?" I asked. "No, Just my family, he returned. I just wanted to talk to somebody about this."

Fred started talking about the catfish pond. "Did you notice something about the lake as you came in?" he asked. I did see some concrete structures in the field but had no idea what it was.

The catfish pond looked like it always did from the highway but what wasn't visible from the road was a circular concrete canal about five feet wide and two feet deep. The water was moving slowly and at a hundred yards intervals air was pumped into the water. Swimming in that canal were hundreds of the biggest channel catfish I have ever seen. They must have averaged three pounds each. (Everybody knows Doc Tebbe lies when it involves fishing; they could be about half that size and still look that big to me)

"Doc, do you have any idea where all those restaurants around the lake get their catfish filets for their catfish dinners?" I was thinking, from fish vendors and maybe the catfish came from Arkansas or Mississippi, but the pride showing on his smile said it all. He not only sold his dressed fish filets to all fourteen restaurants in Celina but in five other small nearby cities. "I've made more money from one acre of catfish raceways than I do milking cows, and telling the truth, I am getting tired of milking cows three times a day." He continued, "My idea is to sell the farm and move to Mississippi to grow catfish, and maybe pigs."

The water in the raceway was warm for a winter day. He explained that a well he drilled three years ago brought up luke-warm water year round, but it was not enough to keep the fish comfortable in the winter, so he had to heat the water. Mississippi conditions allowed growing fish all year round.

Fred had a well thought-out plan that had a good chance of success. It was an impressive project. He made good on his goal of moving to Southern Mississippi and growing pigs until he could get his catfish project running. He also brought a lot of equipment that wouldn't fit into that briefcase he mentioned earlier.

Several years later Fred called me from Mississippi asking if I would be interested in coming down to help him with a problem concerning an infection in his fish the last several weeks.

The weekend trip to Biloxi in the middle of summer was certainly different than I expected. The hot weather assaulted every sensory system in my body. Sweat soaked my clothes day and night.

The rental cars looked like they came from a used car lot. None had air conditioning. A near-vintage pickup truck with the windows open was my transportation of choice.

Daytime temperatures stayed ninety degrees from nine AM to six PM with a relative humidity of ninety percent unless it was raining; then it cooled down to eighty degrees with one hundred percent relative humidity!

Mosquitoes and bugs loved it! It wasn't the perfect place for a summer vacation unless you were a fisherman. That part of our country was a paradise for all kinds of fishing.

Fred met me at the airport to follow him through the woods and swamps to finally reach his fish farming operations near Saucier, Mississippi. Fred grew the catfish there because it was close to custom fish processing and cold storage facilities.

His pig growing location was twenty miles further north and that was where he lived. What a difference from the bayou climate and the pine-wooded hills. Even at that, it was still too hot to grow out pigs for three months in the summer. His problem was with the catfish raceways; concrete canals five feet wide and three feet deep, connecting a complete oval circuit for two hundred yards. We smelled the stench long before we arrived. The raceways were murky, and the fish were distressed.

Catfish farms do not smell ordinarily, but if the bacterial fermentation in the water overloaded the toxins from dead bacteria and decomposing fish "kill-off," it was a terrible smell. His neighbors certainly had to be complaining by now.

A real test of the water in any fish raceway was the ability to see the whole fish in the water and sometimes the bottom. Fred's raceway failed that test miserably.

The fish needed destroying immediately, and the concrete raceways had to be cleaned and dried. If this smelly mess occurred three years later, it would qualify for EPA's first Superfund site!

This was Fred's second time to sanitize his raceways, so he hadn't sold any fish since February. On that occasion, the dead fish were processed (removed the intestines) and ground into dried meat scraps. It made a particularly good source of protein for swine rations at a low cost. He wasn't in business to grow catfish just to make feed for pigs, but it did soften his loss.

Fish farming was not my strongest skill set, but I read about catfish aquaculture and its' challenges before going to solve any problems.

What was involved was the consistency of the feed pellets that were spread over the water surface twice a day, feeding the fish. The pellets were too soft, and they broke apart too soon allowing the crumbs to sink to the floor of the raceway. Within 36 hours this wasted feed lying on the bottom of the raceway was well into very active fermentation and decomposition. Bacteria died off, releasing toxins that made the fish sick and eventually die. The worst smell came from the decomposed dead fish protein.

Back in Fort Recovery, I made rations for Fred's pigs and his dairy herd using premixes of vitamins and chelated minerals to balance the nutrients. He had a small farm grain-milling elevator on his farm in Fort Recovery, and he had it dismantled to bring it to Mississippi. It was set up at the pig farm, but Fred wasn't using it yet. Other things took priority, so Fred mixed all his feed at a local feed mill. He did not have the equipment to make pelleted feed, but the mill he was using did.

Fred's pigs didn't need any help from me, but the fish were in big trouble. We needed to get back to better nutrition using pre-mixed supplements made specifically for catfish into pellets that contained a natural wax with the goal of having a pellet that stayed on the surface longer instead of breaking up. It would take trial runs until the pellets' wax content was perfect. I suggested trying beeswax as the binding substance and advertise that his catfish were "honey-sweet."

Feeding once a day assured the fish were not fed too much because at some point, the fish will not eat all the feed, and the old problem would happen again. Fred was overfeeding the fish in several ways, and what he was feeding the catfish was out of nutritional balance. He fed the fish twice a day because the pellets disappeared by evening, so he fed them again, adding to the overfeeding situation.

Fred was also feeding insects every night. Not just a few insects. Fred had twenty acres on his fish farm. A part of the land contained the water raceways for feeding catfish to sell and five acres of ponds where he grew fingerlings to about six inches long. These he sold to other catfish farmers in addition to what his operation required. That enterprise kept him from going broke.

His hatchery wasn't very big, but his breeding fish were! Some of the females weighed forty pounds (and the bull catfish were almost as big). Each of these females produced 150,000 eggs over twelve years. The eggs developed into "sac-fry" after incubation for seven days.

This part of his fish farming was doing fine. They had a steady diet of insects as well. It turns out that these big "momma catfish" needed the extra protein to make all those eggs, so they were appreciating the way Fred was feeding them. How do you feed insects to a fish? Just get a bug close to a catfish, and it's a "gulp-yum" moment.

Fred had several contraptions made from airboat parts that he had mounted on pillars two feet above the surface of each pond, and on every raceway section, light with a precise wavelength that attracted insects. Behind the propeller and the light was an electric bug zapper.

Fred estimated these fans drew in three to four hundred pounds of insects every night for seven months of the year. The zapped bugs dropped into the water, and the catfish ate them and loved it.

We figured in the insect protein boost into how to formulate the ration the growing fish in the raceways needed. Feeding this natural insect source saved Fred a lot of money for a protein supplement. How did we calculate the impact of feeding insects? I guessed.

When Fred harvested his first fish for meat after this cleanup and ration change, it had been fourteen months since the last fish he sold. I kept in touch with Fred and his boys occasionally, and their system was still working years later. The feed mill changed its pelleting system to Fred's specification and was servicing all the other local growers.

Other fish farms began using the giant bug zappers too. The catfish finished out to an ideal market weight of one and a half pounds in almost three months shorter time than average and seemed healthier than those not feeding insects. A feeding ratio of 1.3 pounds of fish food to make one pound of fish weight is considered excellent feed efficiency. Fred's ratio was 0.8 pound of feed to one pound of fish, not including the insects, which was extraordinary.

The last time I called Fred, he had another problem. "When harvesting the catfish, seagulls and other ocean birds knew a good opportunity for a free meal somehow, and descend upon the farm. "What can we do?" I couldn't think of a solution, so I recommend they ask the Game and Fish Division. They told Fred to harvest at night. Why didn't I think of that?

INVITATION TO WHERE?

Richard Nixon, President of the United States, was the first president to reach out to China with emphasis on trade during the "Cold War" era. Until 1971, there was a lot of energy spent to separate China and The United States in every way.

The Korean War was still a fresh memory for America and China's role in world politics and commerce was hidden behind a wall of secrecy. Add to that; China was a Communist country.

In December, a courier messenger from The State Department extended me an invitation to spend three weeks in China as a guest of the Chinese People, meaning the Chinese Communist Government. The letter demanded one hour to make the decision to accept or decline.

Discussing this with my wife was out of the question. She was at a retreat in Wheeling, West Virginia with her aunt, "Mamie" otherwise known as Sister Alberta, a nun. Disturbing them just would not happen. Dr. Mitchner was present when the courier arrived and volunteered to go in my place. The messenger's response was, "Negative!" My decision to participate was accepted, and the agent took the invitation out of the locked briefcase and handed it to me to sign that the message was affirmed.

There was a lot of information lacking, but apparently, the courier wasn't the person to discuss anything. He closed the briefcase and locked it to his wrist with what looked like handcuffs. He was almost to the door when he said, "An agent will contact you." And with that, he left.

Indeed, a CIA agent contacted me. He was standing outside in the light snow smoking a cigarette waiting for the courier to leave. They passed in the foyer silently, and just like that, he was inside and took off his wet raincoat, then produced his credentials. His name was Helmut and the last name in German.

He saw the confusion on my face and said, "Call me Steve. I'm here to give you a briefing on your possible trip to China this coming spring. First, you need to understand there is only a 50-50 chance of it happening."

The veterinary clinic used to be a bar with attached living quarters and a big room for our dairy management classes, so we went to the quarters where Dr. Mitchner made fresh coffee, and the three of us sat down to talk. The curiosity was killing Dr. Mitchner and me. "Steve" apparently had the answers we wanted.

China was reaching out to the US by hosting six leaders in the food animal veterinary profession in America. The driving force was the constant famine situation. Their population was over 800 million people.

The population numbers were not the cause of famine. Their problem was that their agricultural production was dismal. Since World War II and the Second Sino-Japanese conflict before that, their farming methods reverted to near primitive. The country wanted someone to help bring new and more productive ideas.

China had already made an overture to the US cotton growers who promptly declined the invitation. The US cotton farmers saw that a cheap cotton product in China, linked to China's low cost of manufacturing would wreck the cotton industry in the United States. Veterinarians were their second choice.

"To make the long story short, he said, the Chinese want to pick your minds, and the president says that's OK with him. In return, the US will have bargaining strength to begin commerce between the two countries."

The rest of his briefing was extremely helpful. It would be a safe trip as long as we would behave and not embarrass our country. "No cowboys!" he added. The other five veterinarians that already signed up for the trip included two that would be classified as "cowboys" in that they had big egos and were certainly adventurous. I consider myself on the verge of being a "cowboy."

The agent said, "I am not here to give advice, just information, and the other veterinarians will have the same information."

Dr. Baker, my friend from California, was on that list, so he probably chose whom to enlist. Now that all six veterinarians accepted, the vaccination and testing procedures could begin.

Trying to get recent information about China's agricultural ability was next to impossible. There were no exchanges of ambassadors for years, so China was a mysterious place. Famine and government control were known factors, so we accepted our role was to, "See it when we get there."

There were no reservations about revealing secret information to the Chinese. If we could help, we would gladly put our best effort into the task. Questioning people who spent time in China was not helpful. Veterinarians now, but soldiers who served in China twenty-seven years earlier gave a wretched description of food production and the lack of food.

All talked about watching thousands of people die of starvation and disease. Every comment indicated they doubted there was any improvement during the past quarter century.

I was beginning to feel like a missionary heading into a famine in a far off place armed with nothing but faith in my veterinary knowledge.

Several months passed and I heard nothing from the government. I got all the necessary vaccinations except a few scheduled within thirty days of departure.

The newspapers were hinting of an emissary going to China on a "Good Will" gesture. That sounded pretty singular, and soon it was revealed that a Ping-Pong player would make that trip. I was thinking, "Good luck with the vaccinations buddy, you are going to be so stiff from the shots that the paddle will feel like it weighs fifty pounds!"

A letter with the State Department logo was delivered in my mail late in March. The letter thanked me for volunteering my service to the country. After thorough evaluation, they decided to send an athlete as a good will ambassador. The letter was nine lines, two paragraphs, and it was unsigned.

Maybe some day it would be nice to visit China. A couple of those vaccinations were good for a lifetime.

JUNKETS

Trips to far away and exotic destinations were designed to reward doctors, dentists, and veterinarians for their patronizing the manufacturers' products. Most of the trips Zandy and I were able to enjoy also had a continuing education perk of between five to twenty CE (Continuing Education) credits, certified proof of completed continuing education to use for renewal of licensure.

Dr. Mitchner believed that the trips helped the drug companies free themselves from the guilt for charging far too much for their vaccines and antibiotics.

We were guests of our veterinary vendors about once a year, and Dr. Mitchner had the same opportunity. I seriously doubt we would ever visit places like Bermuda, San Francisco, The Kentucky Derby and Santa Anita Steeplechase, Las Vegas, Miami and The Greenbrier in West Virginia without the help of the drug companies.

One trip stands out because we were the beneficiaries of a very nice shirt. That event occurred on a Pan American flight in February 1971, when we were heading for Venezuela, "The land of perpetual spring." The winter in Ohio was long and dreary, and this was to be a bright spot of the winter. I packed clothes in a hurry and forgot to pack my shirts, and as it is with couples, I caught hell for doing something so stupid.

The man across the aisle heard my wife berating me. He stood up and took his shirt off his back and gave it to me. That man was Governor Love of Colorado. The governor's public relations guy took pictures of the ceremony for the folks back home.

Caracas, Venezuela — The land of perpetual springtime. That sounded so glamorous until looking out from the window seat and watching the mountain looming large and getting too close, too fast!

This flight was my third time as a passenger in a big airplane and with the other two flights being bad experiences in the Army. It scared me to see mountains that moved! The landing was perfect.

We landed at the Maiquetia Airfield, and It was a relief to find the mountain was several miles away even though it still looked immense at three or four thousand feet elevation, rising abruptly from the sea. At least it stopped moving!

So many observations on this trip were mind-bending. How neat was it to watch a small Thorobred racehorse start the journey to fame in a race in Caracas? Canonero II won in an exciting show of speed for such a small horse with a crooked leg. The same horse won the 1971 Kentucky Derby in one of the biggest upsets in horse racing. He also won the Preakness and placed fourth in the Belmont.

The widest boulevard in the world at the time, el Bulevar de Sabana Grande was in Caracas, starting from government buildings and ended a mile south in small narrow dirt streets.

All kinds of vehicles were packed in the boulevard, and I'll bet forty-four years later nothing has changed since, traffic-wise. Traffic lights were meant to stop drivers long enough to allow a street kid, usually six to eight years old, to wash a windshield with a dirty wet towel, then the traffic resumed. Mostly, nobody paid much attention to the color of the traffic light.

Colorful hillsides were a visual treat related to the upcoming election. The houses perched on the mountainsides were painted the color of the occupant's choice for their leader. The presidential contestants provided a different colored can of paint for any resident who voted for him as their president. If their man lost the election, there was a scurry to get the color representing the new president.

People lived all over that mountain, and many grew flowers that went back with our airplane as cut flowers for florists in America. We attended a flamenco dance that started on a blocked-off street at eleven o'clock PM and lasted until breakfast. We rode the cable gondola up and down that scary mountain three times while we visited Caracas.

That was a typical junket, but there was more for that trip. Our continuing education was about a new product to treat worms for cattle, presented by our sponsor, the producer of the medicine. A slide show came up depicting the life cycle of one of the cattle parasites.

The second picture paralyzed me. The picture was the one I sent to this company while I was a freshman in vet school. It showed several blades of grass with dewdrops from the on-campus university pasture containing seven juvenile larvae just out of their egg casings. I took that picture with a close-up magnifying lens on my Rolleiflex camera and developed it in my basement darkroom at the Alpha Zeta Fraternity house.

I sent the picture and the film to this company, and asked for what it was worth for a starving student. There was no reply. They, of course, dismissed me and never paid for a picture used for their advertising for a dozen years.

I asked how many larvae were on the picture that they were proudly rolling out as a new advertising pamphlet. The speaker admitted he didn't know. I told them there were seven and where to look for them. The response was, "That's interesting." That picture was featured on the covers of many agricultural magazines for years until they introduced another parasite product.

The next day the leader of the group asked if there was some way they could make me more comfortable after yesterday's outburst; anything short of admitting the picture was mine. "Oh boy! This will cost you", I thought to myself.

Three years prior, a shipment of thirty-two of the best dairy cows from the Midwest were shipped to Venezuela, with the help of my friend, Brother Bernard from Saint Charles Seminary.

I processed all the testing, identifications, vaccinations, and the International Health Certificates, while Brother Bernard was the person that attended to the cows on their boat trip and beyond to make sure the cows arrived safely and healthy. He would be pleased if I could give him an update.

A trip was arraigned for my wife and four more passengers of my choosing to join me. The thrills began! The airplane was a refitted US warplane to make it a passenger plane. The pilot was a happy fellow who let the passengers take pictures from the cockpit.

We were flying low over a plateau when the world dropped out underneath us. We just passed over the Angel Falls; the highest falls in the world with its plunging river falling more than three thousand feet. We snapped pictures as the pilot turned to get another view when the co-pilot yelled at the pilot to get back to the controls.

We were very close to the falls this time around, getting an airplane wash as we flew through the spray. I thought that maybe they did that on every flight just for excitement.

The ranch was near the falls, and as we dropped into the sea of grass, I was afraid our stupid pilot was lost. There was nothing but grass as far as I could see. The plane banked and headed into the grassy plain again. All of a sudden we were landing on a dirt runway, a smooth landing. The guy did know how to fly that airplane.

The news at the ranch was not the same we got at the agricultural embassy. Yes, someone moved the cows to this location for some unknown reason by an agricultural supervisor. The cows could not survive on the rough grass and soon were dying of starvation and foot and mouth disease.

Not a cow lived, but neither did the man who paid for the venture with government money, not his own. He made enemies, and those kinds of issues were apparently finished quickly in some of these Latin American countries. I was thinking, "This may be the land of perpetual spring, but it had a scary side!"

After refueling, we took off in the night for the 600-mile flight back to the capital. The hulk of a mountain was there to fly into. The mountain looked frightening in the moonlight, but it was in fact, not in the way of a fairly large airport located along the shore that had long smooth runways of concrete.

We certainly had answers for the question, "What did you do on your vacation?"

THE TONIGHT SHOW

Watching Television was a luxury for a busy veterinarian offering twenty-four-hour emergency service for farm animals in rural Ohio. It was a good day if the ten o'clock news at night fit in the busy day, but the Tonight Show at eleven was a great treat and we usually watched it before bed.

Early March in Ohio was the worst time of the year, but this year it was different for us. We planned a Southwest working vacation for the next week. I dedicated three days to take the Arizona Veterinary Board Exam, and three more days to get warm in the Phoenix sunshine.

To keep from burning out or falling into a funk from working the long grueling hours Dr. Mitchner and I took time out periods to rejuvenate our souls. We figured that while we worked such long hours, we would take mini-breaks where one vet disappeared for several days while his partner worked his tail off, alternating back and forth a couple of times a year. That had something to do with sanity vs. insanity. We were looking forward to the week in Phoenix.

The early March evening was particularly nasty. It started with rain that preceded a cold front carrying snow and freezing temperatures The call that came in demanded veterinary care for a cow that delivered a healthy calf earlier in the day without help but several hours later she prolapsed her uterus and was down with "milk fever."

Unable to get up in her struggle, exhaustion took its toll. She was paralyzed, and her inverted vagina and uterus slowly snaked its way through the pelvis to the outside. The owner had this happen before and lost cows with this situation. He was instructed to gather some necessary materials and have them ready for me at the barn when I arrived.

"This is what I signed up for when the decision was made to be a veterinarian," I thought to myself. The fire in the fireplace of our new home in the woods warmed the family room. The weather was beautiful to watch from the cozy reading chair as the new storm turned from rain to swirling snow. I planned to read my current book, Doctor Zhivago for an hour, and then watch television. Five minutes later, I was on the road to take care of a cow with a prolapsed uterus!

Driving conditions were lousy, with high winds and freezing rain mixed with snow, making the roads slippery. In bad weather, it seemed that our practice experienced about one prolapsed uterus a week as long as the inclement weather continued. So far we haven't seen the sun since the beginning of February, and the ten-day forecast promised the same weather to stay.

We had an idea that the prolapsed uterus problem was related to the nutrition of the cow in the last two months of her pregnancy since it usually followed the cow being prostrated by milk fever. We didn't quite figure out what changes had to be made to prevent this costly condition. There was no solace in the fact that nobody else had the answer. The connection between the inclement weather and the increased toll of dairy cow prolapses was noted for years, but the remedy was reclusive. Veterinarians used the word, "stress" to explain the unknown.

Pete Stoffer was a "sometimes" client who called us when he couldn't get his regular vet. He also lived on the fringe of our serviceability of about twenty-five miles from Fort Recovery. Driving in this weather was expected to demand at least half the time for this call.

Pete let me know that in the past, he lost two good cows with prolapsed uteruses and did not want this one to die. I instructed him to keep the cow sitting upright (sternal recumbency) and mainly cover the exposed uterus to keep it warm. We also needed heated water and five to ten pounds of granulated white sugar. I had everything else needed in my truck.

When it involved warming a space in a cold barn, or even outside, the farmer always figured how to get it done. They were much more inventive than any veterinarian.

The dedicated workspace for this job took place in a warm, draft-free stall heated by a kerosene space heater. Dr. Mitchner told me early in my tenure to let the farmer figure out the housing conditions. In twenty-five years of his experience, not one barn burned down because the vet wanted to be warm.

With "milk fever" in a cow, her blood system levels of calcium, phosphorus, and magnesium drop suddenly at the time when the mammary glands begin milk letdown.

Those minerals make their way into the blood system in three ways: first, dietary, or feeds like hay, grain, and supplements that set free the minerals through digestion.

Second, the minerals were indispensable in making milk, but those minerals were constantly being deposited in the bone mass and subsequently were drawn back into the blood stream as needed.

In the third scenario, when the demand for those minerals exceeded the ability of the animal to supply through the first two methods, this deficiency was replaced quickly with an infusion of a fluid supplying all these minerals intravenously.

These three minerals were essential for muscle performance, including the heart, in addition to hundreds of metabolic miracles.

At the barn, I listened to the heart rate and strength of the heartbeat to calculate when to slow down and when to stop giving the IV medication. My unique method was to sit on the cow's shoulder to feel the heartbeat through her bones to the bones in my butt and then transmitted to my brain somehow. That makes sense, doesn't it? I attracted a bit of attention for my unorthodox method, but when I needed four hands to keep the needle in the jugular vein and at the same time hold the IV bottle and monitor the patient, sitting atop the cow made sense to me.

Administering the solution intravenously in every case involving paresis was always the first action. Once the cow had the mineral imbalance stabilized, I started working on the traumatized uterus.

The first duty was to clean the pile of uterus tissue with warm soapy water, followed with a thorough covering with plain white sugar. The sugar coat was gently massaged all over the mass, which sometimes weighed over a hundred pounds, so it required time, usually an hour of hard work.

The sugar on the uterus started the process of osmosis and resulted with the fluid that built up quickly finding its way to the outside of the uterus. This process was similar to sugar on strawberries: soon after sugar application to the strawberries the result was lots of juice and shriveled smaller berries.

This cow took only ten minutes from start to finish to replace the uterus. It took twice as long to give the IV infusion. I was fortunate to get that part finished in so short of time since that was the end of a very long day. My energy was running on fumes!

The calcium, phosphorus, and magnesium injected earlier helped to constrict the uterine muscles, so the animal contributed to the process. Sutures were placed to prevent the uterus from coming out again. With that, the cow was ready to stand. She also received an antibiotic and a tetanus injection.

At that point, it was, "Clean up and go home time." The antibiotic probably wasn't needed because the sugar in the uterus made it impossible for bacteria to live and multiply in that environment.

The icy, slippery road was waiting for me, but I drove carefully. The twenty-five miles to the house took more than an hour, and that was a world slowest record for me. I missed the ten O'clock news, but it didn't matter, a shower took priority. We were still able to watch the Tonight Show.

The Tonight Show host Johnny Carson was introducing my favorite movie star, John Wayne. His films and his greater than life personality were inspiring, to say the least. I heard John Wayne announce that he beat the "Big C" (cancer). Before the host, Johnny Carson could ask the obvious questions about that; The Duke said, "First, I want to talk about something else. My partner, Ben Johnson and I are looking to hire a veterinarian at our 26-Bar Ranch in Arizona."

That got my interest, and suddenly my attention index hit one hundred! My heart was pounding. I felt he was talking to me! John Wayne talked about genetic selection in Hereford cows and bulls and applying that science to the new concept of embryo transfer or embryo transplant. He talked about the impact it would have to speed up better breeding cattle programs all over the world.

He continued, "Now, any of you vets out there just coming home beat up and wanting to turn your career around, give Ben Johnson a call tomorrow morning. I'll be sleeping in." With that, the telephone number for Ben Johnson scrolled across the bottom of the television screen

Zandy was pretty excited, saying, "I'm calling first thing in the morning. I want to go to Arizona!" As far as I remember, there was always an interest in working in Arizona, and I would go there if the right opportunity came, but I had no idea that Zandy also had a dream to live in the Southwest. She said, "This is our chance."

The truth is, I had already heard that the 26 Bar Ranch was planning to start an embryo transfer program. News like that was quick to get around at the Bovine Practitioners Conference that we attended every year.

We woke Ben Johnson up too early. Seven AM Eastern Standard Time in Ohio was five O'clock in Arizona Mountain Time. I apologized, but he was not bothered. He was polite, gracious, and awake. He asked if we could come to Phoenix for several days and meet their team, including John Wayne.

Karma interceded once again. In January I applied to take the Arizona Veterinary State Board Exam, scheduled for next week. Our travel dates and hotel rooms were confirmed. All we had to do is to extend the trip two more days.

Zandy and I discussed the situation to a supportive Dr. Mitchner who was making plans to leave the practice also and enter the Federal Poultry Inspection Program. His war injuries made it difficult for him to continue in large animal practice much longer.

Now was a good time to research the offer if it turned out to be one. Two newly graduating veterinarians (one from Fort Recovery) were already committed to work in the practice and would be starting when they graduated in June.

We were ready to go on Saturday with a flight leaving at eleven AM. At five O'clock AM on departure day we answered the phone to, you guessed it, another prolapsed uterus. The outside temperature was close to zero, and the patient had her uterus frozen to a cement floor — outside!

Thanks to the farmer's ingenuity, the owner had a plastic tent shored up with hay and straw bales. It was almost warm with a space heater blowing hard. The uterus was not frozen to the concrete floor when I arrived.

It was a tricky case as it turned out. The uterus wall had permanent damage by way of three torn spots where another cow apparently stepped on the uterus. Surgical trimming and suturing were required.

It was eight thirty when I got home. Twenty minutes later we were on our way to the Indianapolis, Indiana Airport more than 100 miles from Fort Recovery.

There was little traffic that morning, and I lapsed into daydreaming while driving. Zandy was quiet with thoughts of her own. Driving through the countryside brought back memories of experiences during the last ten years in this part of the country.

We were driving through Lynn, the town hit by one of the most powerful tornadoes in 1965. The village was struggling again, four years after the Palm Sunday tornado. Another hit the town a year ago. Next year with all the buildings replaced, the place will look like new again.

The next town, Lancaster, Indiana, was the home of the largest high school basketball field house in the country. A week ago our family watched the game my nephew played guard for his little high school, scoring forty-three points in a close, but losing the game in the regional semi-finals. That was high school basketball excitement at its' best!

The landscape was beautiful. The trees were carrying a load of ice, decorating the bare limbs, down to the smallest twig. I thought that the scene would make a lovely photograph. "I'll miss this countryside if this trip eventually leads us to Arizona," I said to Zandy.

In truth, I felt like, "Man, was I ever tired of winter!"

We made the airport on time, only to find a snow squall that limited visibility delayed our flight due to severe weather conditions. After an hour waiting in our seats on the airplane, the control tower announced a flight departure window and the plane started moving.

We were the last flight to leave Indianapolis. As the aircraft ascended to an elevation above the clouds, the early March sun finally shone for the first time in a month for us. The passengers cheered, clapped and were thankful there really was a sun shining over Indiana.

I have always believed in Karma. What will be has a reason for happening, good or bad, your choice. The events in the last seven hours and the days proceeding had to be a sign that this venture was destined to turn out well, and chances were good that we would move to Arizona. It felt like Arizona was where we belonged.

I wished that I had that much confidence in passing my state board examination coming up too fast.

Meeting the team Ben Johnson mentioned the week before was an exciting experience. The conference room at The Cowboy Steakhouse was crowded and noisy with enthusiastic, intelligent, and ambitious men with confidence in their success.

Ben Johnson was the most informed person in attendance when the topics were cows, horses, and Arizona. The rest of the personages were doctorates in genetics, nutrition, range management, two movie stars, and one veterinarian, me.

One individual said that he asked several vets active in the bovine veterinary association for possible candidates and my name came up twice as a possibility for the team. That was pretty heady stuff

I immediately saw that some their employees, with training, could fill many of the job descriptions formerly planned for the veterinarian. Their plan was to use embryo transfer technology heavily in their breeding programs. I had no experience in embryo transfer, but I knew Dr. Niedermann from Louisiana who was considered a pioneer in this science. The geneticist knew him as well and believed that hiring him would allow the project to get off the ground earlier.

Immediately, I saw where I could be used better in this operation as a veterinarian. C-section surgery and pregnancy palpation would keep me very busy for three to five days at planned intervals. The recipient cows needed C-section surgeries ninety percent of the time. It was not necessary for a full-time veterinarian during their start-up.

We then agreed they would pay me like any client-veterinarian for my services. Most of my work would be in the Phoenix area taking care of the recipient cows; checking for pregnancy and performing cesarean sections and training the Cowboys at both the ranch in Springerville and the feedlot in Stanfield.

As a special privilege, I would have fishing rights anytime at the 26-Bar Ranch. Fishing rights for the Little Colorado stream that ran through the ranch were no little opportunity. The "Duke" himself designed the landscaping and streambed with an immense amount of dynamite, was the familiar story in the White Mountain community of Springerville.

The Herford Ranch sits at the base of the White Mountains with the ranch headquarters at eight thousand feet elevation. The beautiful setting of the 26-Bar Hereford Ranch wasn't what one expected of a ranch in Arizona. It reminded me of the best of Colorado when it came to nature's beauty.

"You got a deal, Mr. Wayne told me. Now we're going out shopping to get you a real Arizona cowboy hat and a bottle of salt pills. You have to take care of yourself when you're working in that Arizona sun."

John Wayne took me to a cowboy hat shop featuring Stetsons with no price tags. We found the one that suited him. Anything that I got from a celebrity was OK with me. He then handed the hat back to the clerk, and we left the store and hailed a cab.

Within five minutes we were dropped off at a Mexican outdoor Mercado, or marketplace in the parking lot of a Greyhound racing track. The hat booth was doing good business as evidenced by lots of loud talking, exchanging dollars and pesos for sombreros. The hat Mr. Wayne wanted looked just like the one in the hat store. The bargaining began until a boy said, "Papa, that's John Wayne!"

Everything stopped. In Spanish that I didn't understand, the deal was that we got the hat for twenty dollars and for everyone buying a sombrero, John Wayne autographed their sombrero. The merchant wanted my autograph on the sombreros too.

Yes, I treasured that hat! Six months later when working in the hot desert sun in Stanford at the feedlot John Wayne owned, the realization hit me; the Duke set me up with a practical joke! I was wearing the hat for protection from the sun. The hat was a beautiful creation made from dark leather, flat top, just like the design John Wayne fancied for himself in a couple of his movies.

Making movies must be different from sweating in 105 degrees checking cattle for pregnancy. The moisture from sweating loosened the hat on my head, and when we stopped to cool off, the hat dried out, still on my head but farther down, resting on my ears. Soon it was impossible to remove!

The crew had a great time telling me about those "Pilgrim" cowboy hats the "Duke" liked to buy for unsuspecting tenderfoot victims. Talk about hurt; this must be a big man's idea of a joke because it felt like it might decapitate my head at the eyebrows!

That evening a call came from John Wayne asking if I was still alive.

He said, "That advice to take lots of salt tablets to keep from dehydration; you can stop now. I recommend a big salty steak and lots of libation."

The Hopi cowboys at the ranch said that the "Duke" bought them all hats like mine, made of rawhide leather that shrinks when it dries. Han, one of the Hopi Cowboys, said, "You never know when he's serious or pulling your leg. He is an actor, after all."

With two days visiting with the various team members there was no time to cram for the veterinary board exam. When we scheduled the trip earlier, there was no thought of being in Arizona on a different mission.

The exam was scheduled for three days and ended on the last full day we had in the state. Passing the board exam would enable me to pay for and receive an Arizona License to Practice. I spent less than ten hours studying during the last six months, so there was little confidence of passing it.

The night before the test we visited several colleagues to get an idea of what to expect on the test. We learned that if you drink enough Margaritas, it cured the flu. That information still has never helped me in any way over the last two decades. The Board's test questions they were sure to ask would be about poisonous plants of Arizona and it would not be a single answer, but many relating topics. Dr. Dugan's response was, "If it's pretty, it's poison, and if it's green, it has stickers."

Bob Dugan was an Alpha Zeta Fraternity brother from our college days and a good friend over many years. I didn't even get a good night's sleep before the biggest test of my life.

There were more than a few questions about locoweed, so I gave them Dr. Dugan's answer and passed the exam anyhow.

Before we left the next day, Dr. Dugan and his wife Mary Lee met us at Cyril & Maria's Mexican Café for breakfast. Mary Lee asked, "Why don't you think over a proposition we have to offer? Bob is the only veterinarian in his practice, and we haven't been able to hire the professional we want. We haven't visited our families in Ohio since we graduated and this would allow us to get away more often, so please consider working for us when you get settled."

Talk about Karma; Zandy was beaming and shaking her head for Yes. "We'll make it work," she said.

BUSY BEE MILLS

"Colonel" King was a successful farmer by most standards. His herd of Ayrshire dairy cows was a collection of beauty and productivity.

Dairy cow judging for show and genetic selection had a point scorecard to rate the physical characteristics including Frame, Dairy Character, Body Capacity, Feet and Legs, and udder. The ideal cow scored 100. An excellent score was from ninety to one hundred, and it went down from there.

Purebred show cows were royalty, and not many made the excellent range. The Colonel's entire herd averaged 90.7, so the whole herd was excellent.

As good as the herd of cows was, his kennel of Red Tick Hounds was even better. His dogs toured the country winning water races and bench shows. The name of that game was puppies!

Col. King evidently had a natural ability when it came to exceptional breeding stock. He was also one shrewd character, which came in handy in the showing business. His puppies sold for thousands, while my brother-in-law who also had good hunting dogs, sold his pups for twenty dollars.

Colonel King's youngest son Chase brought a two-year-old female hound dog to the clinic one evening to remove a BB from her cervix. The question that I wanted the answer for was, "How in the world can she back into a BB?"

What was said, though, was, "How did you know there was a BB in the cervix," and the answer came back immediately; he admitted to placing it there a year ago. Then he stopped and realized he said something he shouldn't have.

The red dog was in heat, but stuck in her cervix was a copper coated BB that acted as an IUD (intra-uterine device) that was a pretty effective contraceptive. I promised Chase to remove the BB, but it would cost him telling me he whole story. I had ethical issues giving me shivers going up and down my back that I needed to resolve.

He said, 'I figured you might have a problem with it, but this one ends with everybody happy.

As a yearling, "Freckles" was a super prospect to be a breeding dog but she was not yet a proven good hunting dog. The Colonel sold Freckles to a trainer who wanted her as a breeding bitch. (In the dog of reproduction camp, a female is a "bitch, " and a male dog is a "dog," so if it's OK, we will use those terms).

Greg, the trainer, planned to put special effort to make her a complete package as a well-bred hunting dog, which would place her pup's value over her reproductive years somewhere around a hundred thousand dollars.

After two breeding possibilities to get pregnant, she never conceived. Col. King figured that if Freckles turned out as a superb hunting bitch as well now that Greg spent a year training her, he might get her back cheap.

He called Greg saying, "Greg, I heard that you'd had problems getting Freckles to conceive. I'll tell you what we can do. Send her back to us, and we'll give you another pup of your choice as an exchange for no charge." At that point, the Colonel had twenty-five thousand dollars worth of training for free if Freckles became a National Champion Field Trial dog.

Greg sent Freckles back to the Colonel a week before our meeting at the vet clinic, and now she was in early heat, ready to breed within a week. Suddenly, that little BB was a problem. Greg decided that he would rather trade Freckles for "Jackson," a littermate of Freckles with two years of showing and having sired pups that were on their way as good hunting prospects. He would rather have a dog instead of a bitch, and he wanted Jackson as an even trade.

Also, Greg saw the BB scam coming. Chase said he thought it was Greg who told his dad about using a copper plated BB as a contraceptive in the first place and his dad just forgot who it was that disclosed to him about the BB thing.

This complicated story was still swirling in my head with all this, wondering if another big tale followed, when Freckles dribbled a blood clot from her vagina. Freckles gave a little push and discharged the clot with a rusty BB on the top!

Now things were starting to fall into place as to what ethical course to take. There was a little less liability of compromising my values. I flushed the vaginal remnants of copper and iron from the BB, clearing the way for conception if they bred Freckles. They did breed her, and she whelped thirteen puppies of which eleven survived.

In the future, these people needed watching. They seemed to be one notch sharper than their adversaries in business. Next time it might be me getting the short end of a bargaining agreement.

It wasn't very long after the episode with Freckles that Chase stopped at the clinic for a chat. He had a business idea to discuss with me in confidence. Their family also owned a small feed mill south of Geneva, Indiana that they wanted to sell. The little feed mill practically closed about a year ago.

The thought that the feed mill could fill a need in our nutritional part of our practice never was considered with all the recent growth taking all our spare time (and time for creative thinking). We were in the process of buying Dr. Mitchner's interest in the practice and starting two new associate veterinarians.

All of a sudden, the idea of owning a feed mill to complement our nutrition programs made sense. The possibilities of linking that service to the herd health concept was a genius stroke, so yes, now it made sense. Remembering my previous dealings with the family alerted my brain for danger signals and steeled me to listen to what they had to offer carefully.

It turned out that the two sons had other interests after a terrible year of low prices for their turkey operations. They decided to quit the turkey business for good. Also, Chase was allergic to bees, and the bees were the last straw that prompted him to sell the mill.

He told me the feed mill had a huge population of honeybees, and the mill in the middle of a small village in the Limberlost was a liability because of the bees. The citizens were complaining to the Jay County Health Department. Past efforts with an apiarist trying to move the swarm were not successful. On two occasions, neighbors ended up in the emergency room for multiple stings.

and then he would harvest the honey. That took two weeks. Next, he replaced the siding. We agreed to pay for the materials. With the siding finished, we already had a skeleton crew of workers cleaning the dusty mill and getting ready to start operations. In fact, the wheat and oats harvest was coming in, and the mill was already paying for itself.

The bees never returned.

In the first two years, that feed mill was pure magic! By the second month, we were delivering custom feed for our preventive health dairy programs, two pig feeding yards, four sow/pig operations and one cattle feedlot with 400 steers. By the end of the year, the mill paid for itself, and I was able to finish paying Dr. Mitchner for his share of the practice with my profits.

The new vets were awesome. As a starter, they were capable and well trained for their new jobs. They loved their work. If having two more veterinarians in practice was supposed to give me more spare time, that part failed miserably. Dr. Mitchner had already left the practice for service in the federal poultry inspection program in Germany. It was a perfect fit for his talents, and the meat inspection service gained an outstanding veterinarian.

My days had three parts: one six to ten hours doing veterinary calls, six hours tending to the feed mill and herd health, and the remainder to sleep and enjoy my family. That schedule was often broken, but never in favor of the sleeping part.

"Burning out" was recognized and fought, but the condition continued to grow. The challenges of the feed milling and grain marketing were wild rides and "crash learning" lessons. Losing control of the practice wasn't a concern because the young vets embraced a busy arena and they were able to handle it.

The offer to sell the practice to the two veterinarians if they were interested stirred excitement with them, and yes, they were Interested.

Buying and selling grain commodities on the Chicago Mercantile Stock Exchange was also called the "futures" market. It was a way to protect the selling price of various commodities at a future date. Futures trading was a concept new to me. It was legal, very complicated, and it worked.

There was just as much opportunity for the farmer growing the crops to sell their grains for "future" sale dates of delivery. The key to success was having a storage facility large enough to hold in this instance, soybeans, for six months until delivery of the actual commodity on the due date. A four-year-old facility of two large grain silos was available to lease, so we put that to use.

Storage capacity was where the big bucks were made in grain trading; and lost! Our first year into trading was lights out successful! Our second year wasn't. When it was time to quit, I never turned a trade again.

My family was the last to get my attention. Zandy was a stranger to me with her mood swings from the stress. She wanted me to be a success, but the price was too much.

We had talked about moving to Arizona. We visited the state, took and passed the Arizona Veterinary Board even with no time to prepare for it, and by September 1972 we moved rather suddenly. I felt like Fort Recovery was getting rid of one of their "crazies, " but I also felt relief as the family vibes continued getting better to the point of "Happy" again.

Thinking we were financially secure, Yogi Berra's quote, "It ain't over till it's over" was forgotten. We had a practice that I planned on selling to the two new veterinarians when they were ready. In the meantime, they leased the practice from me. Two silos of dried soybeans already paid for and ready to make a delivery on December 20 was like a fortune in the bank. Little of that plan came true.

We left Fort Recovery at the end of August in style, thinking that "Karma" had dealt us a good hand. When we came to the town a little over ten years earlier, all our possessions fit into the trunk of our car.

Our move to Arizona was different. The moving van was huge and stuffed full of ten years of our life. We followed in our Ford van from the clinic. The new vets each had their custom truck made for veterinarians and didn't need my van.

The day after we arrived in Arizona I went to work under the same circumstances faced ten years earlier. The family of Dr. Dugan left for their first vacation in twelve years, and they returned when they got tired of traveling.

It was a different situation, however; the two-way radio worked. That was good since a lot of his clients lived over a hundred miles from Buckeye, where Dr. Dugan had his practice. Doing relief work for Dr. Dugan while he was away was pure joy for me. I felt a happy thrill every morning just driving through the countryside and wondering what kind of new adventure was waiting for the day. I was never disappointed and often thought I should have started my vet career in Arizona.

Did I mention the heat? The month of September was an orientation in survival at 110 degrees, day after day, but the evenings and early mornings were spectacular! The heat eventually moderated into October and November, but it was still summer to me. If I missed the cold weather, my two to three days at the 26-Bar Ranch in the White Mountains getting cows ready for embryo transfer once a month reminded me to think warm. They had heavy snow at 8,000feet elevation!

In late November a call came from my feed mill manager, Brian, with the news that somebody stole the soybeans at the Olding silos and what they didn't take they left rotting in the snow. The bank held those soybeans as collateral for a short-term loan to cover "margin calls" on my soybean contracts. And the bank panicked.

Before I could leave, I received a demand for immediate payment by summons, supported with receivership of the feed mill business. They would simply take over all the assets of the Busy Bee Mill, including the futures contracts on twenty thousand bushels and another seventy thousand bushels we bought during harvest. We were set to sell all the beans on December 20th. I paid for all these soybeans at harvest time, except 5%, which I borrowed from the bank, hence their involvement.

The problem for me was that there were nowhere near ninety thousands bushels of soybeans to clear the bank's demands.

I recalled the sage advice, "Don't place all your beans in one silo." The beans were mostly gone, but more than enough were left behind to pay off the loan. What I didn't have anymore was my confidence in the integrity of banks.

My lawyer filled me in on the facts and summed it up succinctly: The criminals were a sophisticated organization involved in stealing semi trucks, altering the VIN's on truck motors, and selling the stolen contents at auctions all over the Midwest in little communities. They sold everything in three hours and left town.

Stealing the soybeans was like picking the "low fruit." They had lots of trucks at their disposal, so they lined up enough to empty the silos down to twelve feet. Locks on the gravity chute were shot off, and the beans started pouring into the train of grain-hauling trucks without stopping. According to the neighboring reports, the thieves loaded their trucks in little more than a few minutes, and they drove off, spilling beans on the ground until the next truck pulled into place. Neighbors recalled that there were trucks at the silos for about two hours on Thanksgiving Day. Two other grain elevators lost their stored soybeans on that holiday weekend in the same manner.

What happened to the beans? The FBI took two years to finalize their investigation like the attorney said they would. The soybeans ended up in Japan with the help of crooked managers of a major grain company. Along the way, the thieves sold those futures contracts for sixteen thousand bushels, so there was a paper trail for the FBI to follow.

The truck stealing syndicate was busted, and three men went into federal prisons. One was a farmer from Salamonia that I did not know. He was charged with tampering truck engine identification. The other two were from a stock brokerage company for knowingly trading stolen soybeans. The kingpin from the grain company escaped FBI scrutiny; neither was anybody else regarding the truck-stealing ring as far as I know.

The truckers who lost their rigs were mostly insured, and the young man who was my assistant manager turned crook was found in a field near Viewpoint, naked, wrapped in barbed wire and castrated. Immediately after neighbors cleaned him up and gave him some clothes, he disappeared. Did I have anything to do with that? No, but thoughts pretty close to what happened to him did come to mind.

My lawyer advised me to let the bank take care of the dispersal of the assets under the terms of receivership. Forget the loss. "From what I know about you, you are a good veterinarian. Stay in Arizona, and you'll have a good chance to make a new life; something everybody wishes for but never gets." Good advice.

The good news was that a hard lesson was learning things about myself that were positive. The unfavorable news was that we learned Zandy had Lupus of the brain and liver. The rheumatologist predicted that it would probably be a long-term disease, but both of those forms of Lupus were lethal, and there was no cure, only relief with cortisone.

VAQUEROS AT PAINTED ROCK

Gila Bend was on my mind for the past week. As the new vet helping Dr. Dugan in Buckeye, Arizona with his practice while he was on vacation, the work was exciting so far. The scheduled ranch call to geld 27 horses and perform a fertility check on an old Longhorn-cross bull at a desert corral twenty miles west of Gila Bend bothered me.

That might be out of my league, certainly out of my comfort zone. No vet ever gelded 27 horses, then collected semen from a recalcitrant old bull and lived to brag about it!

At 5:30 in the morning in September it was already at least warm. The forecast for the high temperature for Gila Bend was to reach 110 degrees by afternoon. "Never fear, the Pilgrim hat The Duke gave me in March will keep me in the shade."

Twenty-seven horses to geld! Three in a day would be a lot. Dr. Dugan called me the night before to give me some tips on gelding horses at the remote desert cattle operations. I talked to my brain, begging it to remember all the stuff he said.

The drive to Painted Rock was the best part of my day, with the sun at my back just thinking about coming up. The drive through the Buckeye irrigated fields smelled fresh, and the western sky finished turning a clear bright blue. The eastern sky with the sun rising was all shades of pink to red. The last cotton field transitioned to the raw desert with a red morning sky. It was beautiful, even in the rear view mirror.

I passed through sleepy Gila Bend and headed west through five miles of more cotton fields. The turn off Highway 85 came up where a sign indicated the direction to the second largest lake in Arizona. That didn't make sense. Arizona sure had a lot of unexpected sights. There were fifteen more miles down this dusty, rough road to Painted Rock Reservoir, named after numerous petroglyphs etched in stone surfaces by long forgotten human beings living along the Gila River over a thousand years ago.

A dusty old white pickup was parked under a mesquite tree up ahead. The driver waved me down and motioned to follow him.

Over the fifth hill the headquarters of the ranch and the lake with water as far as I could see facing west was a spectacular sight. It took a few minutes to take in the beautiful view. I was wondering what kind of fishing the lake held, but we had work to do.

The driver introduced himself as Manuel. That was the only word I understood by the polite Mexican cowboy (Vaquero).

The Boss spoke English with a German accent. He wasn't a pleasant man, but he fit in the desert, and he knew his business. Dr. Dugan said Bruno was likable and that he was quite a character. Apprehension set in. The guy looked as tough and harsh as the desert behind him.

At the corrals, there were indeed 27 young stallions, some six or seven years old. All were relatively small. Bruno grunted, "These cowboys are Mexicans. They like to call themselves "Charros" and they are damned good at working cattle with their little horses. You vill zee ven via bekommen gehen", which I translated quietly in my head, "You'll see when we get there."

We moved the vet truck to the center of the corral where the vaqueros led the horses in one at a time. Everything we needed was in the mobile vet truck. In two minutes, Bruno laid out in Spanish to his vaqueros how we would castrate 27 horses in two hours. He explained, "Because after two hours even my vaqueros won't work in the heat out here, so let's get going!"

There were ten vaqueros; all lived with horses their entire life and it showed as they guided the wild range horses through their surgeries. The procedure needed to have everything finished in two and a half minutes on each horse.

The sedation was a single intravenous injection of Succinylcholine that would immediately immobilize the horse. For a short time, the muscles were completely relaxed except for the heart muscle. That meant the horse could not breathe until the medicine wore off.

off to release the gate stuck in the bull's horns. Somehow they got it loose, but now there was a bull that might be aggressive, three men on the ground and one on his horse. The gate was wide open.

Anything could have happened, and most of it would be bad. Black Bart picked the triumphal hero route, though: He sauntered through the open gateway into the hundred square miles of the Sonoran Desert and was soon out of sight.

I asked Bruno what this year's calf crop looked like. He said that most look like that big black bull. 'Well, I suggest that until they start looking like something else, let him do his job without those semen checks. To tell the truth, having him break out into the desert makes me feel better. Somebody is going to get killed trying to collect semen from that bull". Bruno admitted he had no idea how we intended to collect semen from Black Bart. He said that he was just waiting to see what the doctor would do.

I told Bruno about a study at the bull evaluation station in Ohio that came to the conclusion that the diameter of the scrotum is the most accurate indication of fertility in bulls and that nobody needs to crawl beneath the bull with a tape measure. It can be assessed by a game sighting monocular to determine all dimensions from seventy-five yards.

As we were finishing up, Bruno asked what the charges for the day's services were. "How much do you charge per hour?" he asked. I answered, "That's up to Dr. Dugan when he gets back." Bruno probably thought it would be a lot cheaper to pay by the hour.

When Dr. Dugan got back from vacation, we had a discussion about what happened at Painted Rock. Bruno was in to pay his bill, and he had some things to relate to Dr. Dugan about his new associate and his work at the ranch.

"You gelded 27 horses in an hour and a half. Did you?" asked Dr. Dugan in astonishment. "Well, more like two and a half hours, why? Did I do something wrong?" I asked. "No, no, he replied, I've never heard of anybody doing that. That's incredible! It would take me two days to geld that many horses, and that would be bragging!"

Evidently, Dr. Dugan and Bruno came to an agreement on a reduced veterinary bill. Every horse recovered with no complications, so Bruno was pleased enough to ask for that German vet next year. 'He's not from

Germany, Dr. Dugan replied, but he speaks a little bit of German. We're fraternity brothers from college, and we both graduated from the same veterinary school. He spent two years in Germany while in the Army."

"By the way, he said, Bruno left two cases of Lowenbrau beer from his native city, Munchen and I'm half way through mine. Yours is in the staff room refrigerator". There was also a kilo of bratwurst, frozen, also from Munchen. "He is quite a character, Dr. Dugan said, did he tell you he was a German prisoner of war in the 40's and came back to Phoenix after the war?"

BASQUES IN ARIZONA

It's official that the word "Arizona" is a Basque term meaning "the good oak tree" taken from the name of a ranch settlement, La Rancha del Arizona in what is now forty miles southwest of Tumacacori, Arizona.

"Then" was in the 17th century. There are other communities named Arizona throughout the US and Latin America as far away as Argentina, and they all have a Basque connection. It is no surprise that the oldest inhabitants of Europe would be a part of the Spanish explorers led by Jesuits who were, you guessed it, most of the Spanish explorers of the American Southwest were Basque.

Raising sheep in Arizona the old way was something almost every Arizona resident and their visitors forty years ago encountered along the highways of the state. Visitors and residents enjoyed the picturesque sight of hundreds of sheep moving along their century-old trails to and from the winter pastures in the Phoenix area and the mountain grazing grants.

Waiting fifteen minutes while usually a single herdsman and one or two Border Collies moved the flock of sheep across the highway was treated as a refreshing reprieve.

The first trails in the New World Arizona were the Native American trade footpaths. The Spaniard soldiers followed and marked their way through the perilous land by etching the Cross on rocks along the way. The Spaniards and the Basque among them brought livestock and agriculture to scattered and protected presidios in the seventeenth century.

Two hundred years later, it still was not safe to travel in Arizona until the late eighteen hundreds with the Army posts scattered all across the newly designated Arizona Territory. The first rudimentary roads became heavily used by settlers, miners, and by migration of the descendants of the earlier Basque agriculturists from the south.

It was the Basque sheep and cattle herders who carved trails from pasture to pasture over long distances. Those trails became the roadways and railroad lines before Arizona statehood in 1912.

Four decades later, an Interstate Highway parallels the old sheep trails. The migration of sheep was a common occurrence. Today the number of flocks grazing the traditional trails is considerably less, but information is available about where and when to find these sheepherders by contacting ADOT (Arizona Department of Transportation).

Alfilaria is a wildflower that also happens to be very nutritious for sheep and cattle. The Basque sheepherders brought the seeds of alfilaria to Arizona from the Mediterranean area sometime in the latter part of the nineteenth century.

As the sheep moved up to the northern mountains, the sheepherders scattered the alfilaria seeds in likely spots to sprout and grow. The next spring the sheep grazed the plants with its seeds and moved on. For the next several days the sheep droppings fell to the ground, full of alfilaria seeds and those seeds sprouted and grew through the summer rains.

By 1972 when we moved to Arizona, a favorite excursion for the Valley residents was to drive to the areas with spectacular wildflowers lending grace to the naturally spectacular scenery. It was the alfilaria that provided the pale blue band of color, sometimes a mile wide, and blooming for many miles along the old sheep trails.

A hundred and twenty years after the alfilaria was introduced a few Basque sheep companies still drive their sheep up the trails in the spring, but the sheep usually make the late fall journey back in a three-hour ride in a livestock truck.

Many of my neighbors in Litchfield Park were Basque sheep and cattle operations owners. As young men recruited from the Pyrenees Mountains between Spain and France, they started as the sheepherder in charge of a flock. The rancher issued a burro or sometimes a mule, camping gear, and a couple of dogs for the young sheepherder to train by the end of the season.

Food and medicine dropped off at bunkhouses sustained both animal and man.

It was a lonely life, but better than back in Europe. They became naturalized citizens and eventually grew into ownership of their own sheep companies, raised their families, and hired young Basques from Europe to herd their sheep.

These old guys congregated at the Sundowner's Hotel and Café in Goodyear every morning. Everybody in the area associated with agriculture was invited for gossip, breakfast, or just coffee and story telling.

The hotel reserved a set of tables and booths for the "Ag" guys from six in the morning to noon. I think the unwritten rule was, "If you had no gossip or reliable news, breakfast was served at another table."

My favorite time to drop in for breakfast was between my large animal morning calls and the small animal appointments. Sometimes I didn't smell so good, but my friends tolerated me as authentic "Ag."

One of my first calls working for Dr. Dugan was to help stitch up sheep injured in their paddock. A pack of dogs jumped the fence into the compound overnight and chased the herd of three hundred sheep. Many sheep died from being suffocated on the bottom of a pile of animals smashed against the fence. The dogs bit perhaps fifty sheep that needed to be clipped, cleaned, and sutured.

The sheep were recently trucked in from the high meadows north of Flagstaff where the grazing season was over due to freezing weather at elevations of eight to nine thousand feet.

In Buckeye, September was still summer, and warm weather was screwworm weather. The Screwworm fly was a bad actor! This particular year had an outbreak of screwworm infestation and Buckeye was the epicenter of the epidemic.

The surgeries were mostly minor, but just a scratch attracted the screwworm fly to lay 400 eggs in each of four different settings. The female fly deposited her sticky eggs next to the broken skin. In 12 hours the eggs hatched into larvae that crawled into the wound and began feeding. The larva had the equipment to eat its way into viable flesh. Within five days, the larva grew into the mature larva stage and crawled out of the now much larger opening. The gorged larvae dropped to the ground and developed into the cocoon or pupae stage.

Eight days later the cocoons hatched into adult sexually active flies, looking for a mate and the female deposited her eggs within two days of mating. (Actually the male fly was interested in only mating; the female was interested in both.) The entire life cycle completed itself in a little more than two weeks.

The problem was that just one female fly infested four animals and without intervention, those four sheep died. In the process, 1600 new screwworm flies survived, and three weeks later, the 800 fertile female flies had the opportunity to kill several thousand sheep or cows.

It was possible for one screwworm fly to kill four animals, so they were an important parasite, much worse than just a pesky fly. The cost of this pest in the livestock business had years when losses ran into the billions.

Treatment for the injured sheep went farther than suturing. The fleece required shearing away from the wound, any eggs visible, were scrubbed vigorously. A covering of pine tar was smeared for five inches around the original wound. If the larvae were feeding, it was imperative to remove every one of them manually. Then the pine tar was smeared into the wound. Every animal in the flock was carefully inspected for injuries daily during an infestation.

The Basque community turned out to help on this flock and gathered forces again when more outbreaks happened, as this flock did about three weeks later.

Technology provided a tool for eradication. Researchers knew that the screwworm mates a single time, so the federal Agricultural Research Service propagated millions of screwworm flies and exposed the larvae to 2,500, to 5,000 roentgens of radiation, rendering both sexes sterile without disrupting their mating behavior.

Airplanes released the sterile flies over the infested areas. A minimum of a thousand sterile flies was released per square mile once every three weeks. The sterile males mated with native females, and sterile females mated with intact males, resulting in sterile eggs that developed no further.

The irradiated fly program was a spectacular answer to the problem. One dropping of sterile flies would not be enough to stop the screwworm parasite immediately. Subsequent airborne droppings continued for as long as even a single confirmation of screwworm infestation was reported.

Another wave of screwworm surfaced in 1977, and by 1979 Arizona, California and Mexico were declared screwworm free. The facility in Texas produced 75 million radiated flies a week to be spread year round in the warmer zones of these states and Mexico.

It isn't fair to label this story about the Basque in Arizona and piggyback the outbreak of a world-class monster parasite. In my experience, every sheep operation and many of my cattle ranchers were Basque.

I have fond memories of the Basque cattlemen in the San Juan Baptiste area in California where we had our embryo transfer project in the eighties. We bought our ranch from a Basque gentleman; all our neighbors were Basque, and when we needed help to work a lot of cows during our Anaplasmosis episode, the Basque men came to work hard from very early morning to three o'clock in the afternoon. Their families would then come over to our ranch, and the women started their grills and cooked up a feast. The men, of course, started drinking.

After the barbecue of everything from Santa Rosa steak tip to roasted pig to steelhead salmon and more was served, then came some of the best desserts anywhere. Even their great tasting bread was almost a dessert.

Randy's wife (Randy was our embryo transfer project manager) brought a radio out to the patio for music for dancing. The party lasted until midnight with singing, dancing, and talk. The next morning the men were back, ready for a hard day of work. There was no mention of being paid for all that hard work. Neighbors worked together, and our crew donated their share of work at neighboring ranches.

Randy made friends in the neighborhood also by giving away smoked hams and bacon sides previously owned by the many wild pigs he bagged as they came through our ranch on their way to the walnut groves. Throughout the summer, the smokehouse had a dozen smoked hams hanging at any given time.

Those nasty pigs were causing problems for the whole community and had to be thinned out. The seasonal hunt tag for wild pig was good for all year and cost two dollars with no limit on the number of pigs killed.

The role of the Spanish explorers in the New World depended on the tough Basque priests, mariners, and soldiers. As explorers and as pastoral agriculturists they were leaders in survival and taming the lands they discovered. As somewhat a cattleman, I am impressed that these were the successors of the same people who first tamed wild cattle to serve humans 10,000 years ago.

Dairies in the Desert

Milk production from Arizona dairies was a surprisingly big business when our family moved to Arizona in 1972. Practically all of Arizona's dairies were located around Phoenix, so we were located within an area with a sizeable dairy industry with very large dairies.

The west side of Phoenix area was where the agricultural activity was a thriving irrigated copy of the California valleys. The opportunity for my practicing dairy and beef cattle with a sideline of equine work was tempting, as opposed to having a mixed practice with small and large animals.

The problem with strictly working outside with large animals exclusively in Maricopa County was the heat for six months of the year. Not many veterinarians were able to stand the rigors long enough to make it a career. A decision had to be made sometime within the next two or three years regarding spending time treating dogs and cats in air-conditioned comfort. My decision drifted toward comfort.

Ten years in a predominantly dairy practice in Ohio was a good experience and gave me the skills that worked into the kind of veterinarian the Arizona dairymen were seeking. The opportunity to work with milk cow management, along with the introduction into the work with beef cow embryo transfer gave me the chance to build a niche practice; perhaps even a busy one.

It was no surprise that the key to building a dairy or beef cattle clientele required long hours in the heat of the day palpating cows for pregnancy. Only a few vets excelled in this skill. I was one who could, but that's not something to brag about, Dr. Dugan advised me to pick the herds that I would be comfortable to work with for the rest of my career. He told me, "They will be some of your best friends for life."

The dairy herds were much larger than they were back in Fort Recovery. On the west side of Phoenix, there were probably thirty herds averaging 2,000 milking cows. In Ohio, farmers managed dairies. Business managers with college degrees directed Dairies In Arizona. A dairy was an investment of millions of dollars set on a piece of real estate of thirty acres or less.

I left Dr. Dugan's practice to finalize the sale of the Fort Recovery practice to the two young vets and to sell the house in Ohio. Matters in Ohio demanded my presence to close out my old practice. The two young vets went from leasing a veterinary business in Fort Recovery to owning it.

The Buckeye practice of Dr. Dugan in Buckeye Arizona took on a new graduate of Colorado State who was a local young man with lots of relatives in Buckeye. When I settled everything in Ohio and came back to Arizona to stay, I started my practice in nearby Avondale.

It was the dairy and beef work that sustained my family. Gradually a small animal clinic was built, and that business grew. Half of my time was devoted to treating dogs and other pets (and cooling off) in the clinic while large animal calls took several hours in the early morning. I provided twenty-four-hour emergency service for both venues.

A dairy veterinarian in Arizona had to practice herd health maintenance. The routine jobs of delivering calves, minor surgery, and treating for milk fever was the responsibility of trained dairy workers. Emergencies still called for a veterinarian.

As a veterinarian, my job was to stay on top of the nutritional challenges, examine the reproductive systems of every cow at least six times a year, and to use production data for decision making.

It was here in Arizona I learned what caused all those nasty prolapsed uteruses. I repaired only five prolapsed cows in the next 20 years.

The reason for all the prolapsed uteruses in Ohio was stress induced along with the calcium and magnesium severe deficiency in the cow's ration the weeks before having her calf and in particular the last week before giving birth.

For several months the cows were on a precise ration for "dry" cows.

We simply started feeding the milking cow ration instead of the "dry cow ration" for that extra boost of minerals in the last two weeks before calving.

We had to know how much milk production to expect for the cow when she "freshened," or has her calf, since producing a lot of milk suddenly depletes the blood calcium and other minerals. Supplemental feeding these minerals in the chelated form made them available quickly.

My job was to know more about managing the health of the herd than the owner or manager did, and in the end, this team made the herd more profitable. I loved my work. Most of my days started very early, especially in the summer when the mid-day temperatures verged on dangerous. Palpating cows for pregnancy started at daybreak at the latest. Three hours of checking cows held in stanchions and released in groups of thirty took care of from one hundred fifty to two hundred cows.

Dehydration could sneak up on anyone working in temperatures over one hundred degrees. There were times perspiration ran into my boots and spilled over. By drinking much more water at frequent intervals, I could maintain hydration and keep on working. Dehydration was a dangerous and career stopping situation. I found my dream job and did not want to lose it by carelessness.

John Wayne had it right with his advice, "Eat steaks with salt and plenty of libations." Our family and friends frequently visited an excellent steakhouse near Buckeye called "The Original Cowpuncher" with a bigger than life billboard along Highway 85 depicting a Longhorn bull. There was no question about that bull's fertility!

Many of the dairies were located next to one of the river bottoms of the county for some good reasons. Drilling for potable water along the river aquifer usually came up with the volume of water that met the needs of a dairy.

The disadvantages were coyotes, rattlesnakes, mosquitos, Gila Monsters, and occasional mountain lions lived in those washes. I stepped on a Gila Monster weighing about twenty pounds when verifying the ear tag identification on a cow early in the morning. It was a good idea to watch where you stepped.

Unexpectedly, he locked his jaws into my boot, knocking me off balance and for a horrendous few seconds, the critter was twisting around on my stomach, chewing my boot. He was thirty-one inches long. We sent him back to the Gila River marsh.

I keep calling this animal a male, but I'm not so sure what sex it was. The only certain way to determine the sex of a Gila Monster was to perform an ultrasound to show ovaries or testes. This one was huge and stubby, and my gut feeling was that he was a stud. He was too ugly to be a lady Gila Monster!

Few rivers in Arizona had water running, at least on top of the riverbed, but there was underground water that came close to the surface. For desert animals that burrow, the sub-surface moisture was their lifeline. The Gila River had water year round in the Phoenix area and for miles downstream all the way to the Colorado River in Yuma, thanks to the reclaimed city's used water.

Someone has to say it; It does rain in Arizona, even in the deserts, and when it did, the rushing water in the arroyos and streams were a frightening sight. An hour after a flood, the water was gone. A substantial portion disappeared into the riverbed sand, and the rest seemed to run until it got tired.

Dairies used a lot of water and on the west side of Phoenix. It all came from wells drilled down to the aquifers of the rivers. A water conservation trend made headway recently among the larger dairies where they processed the wastewater to the degree that it was suitable for recharging the aquifer, and the waste solids were used to generate energy.

The smaller dairies have always used the manure to fertilize their fields or sell it to someone who wanted to use it for something like compost or fuel to run an electric generator. One large dairy installed an Imhoff generator that collected methane gas from manure to power an electric generator on the property, providing all the electricity for the facility and sometimes sold the excess to the power company.

In all my variety of animal care, being the provider of veterinary skills, I felt more fulfilled as a dairy practitioner in the large dairy herds in Arizona. I enjoyed the relationship with the dairy manager who was a partner, friend, and the purveyor of some of the most creative answers to the challenges that pop up every day. My task was to be as creative as the manager. As a million dollar business in all cases, the veterinarian was a partner and as somebody intelligent and helpful. If the vet failed in those tasks, he risked losing his job.

Some vivid memories of night calls on dairies and range cattle calls ought to be told, like the time I carelessly put my hand on top of a rusty steel pipe on a dairy near Buckeye, and yes, this was along the Gila River bank.

The Holstein cow had milk fever paralysis, and the owner said that he was not able to help the cow by himself.

The twenty- five-mile trip on a scorching day brought me to a corral some distance from the dairy itself. The cow was lying on her side with her legs straight out. I had to look twice to make sure she was still alive.

The owner set up a shade for the cow, but the unfortunate animal needed more than that, and she needed it immediately. The first thing was to get her in sternal recumbency (resting on her sternum with her legs tucked under her) and keep her in that position.

For that, I needed a rope, and my truck was a quarter-mile walk both ways. I could not find the driveway to get to the dry cow corral and had to walk through part of a shoulder-high cotton field.

A lariat lying stretched out along the outside of the pipe corral saved me from a difficult hike, so it was put to use to make a makeshift halter to pull her head up and around to her side. A log about four feet long outside the corral by a shed was the perfect size to place it next to her back so she wouldn't lay flat again. At last the intravenous injection of calcium to correct her deficiency was finally ready to infuse intravenously.

As I went through the gate to pick up my case with the milk fever treatment, my hand gripped the top of the gate with my fingers inside the pipe. I felt a sting on my index finger. A two-inch long scorpion wiggled like a catfish with its tail stuck in the end of my finger, pumping away with the venom pulsing in my finger Feeling like fire!

The immediate need to get this medicine into the cow before she dies was paramount in my mind, but at the moment, the venom was doing some strange things to my body. At first, the sting was like a bee sting, but then the hot sensation started moving up my arm and changed from hot to electric shock. I felt it moving to my shoulder, then to my chest.

The concern about how it could affect the heart because that was the direction it was heading, struck raw fear. The constriction in my lungs made it hard to breathe. "Take it easy" I scolded myself. That sensation was adrenaline making its presence. "Just relax and conquer the fear and the body will take care of this," I kept telling myself. Immediately, my heart slowed down from its frantic pace.

As my heart headed back to a reasonable pace, the hot feeling started migrating back through the shoulder and down my arm to my finger, which continued to hurt until I had a chance to put some ice on it.

My clothes were soaking wet. At least now the only concern was the finger. Then I remembered the cow propped up and not getting the injection that was needed.

The ordeal sapped my energy, but it returned finally, and I was able to finish the intravenous injection. The cow had taken only half the bottle of calcium before the cow's heart started to pound, a signal that indicated for me to stop the calcium. My patient's condition had worsened and could not move her legs at all.

"So what's wrong Big Girl?" I asked the weakened cow, but she didn't answer. Pinching her neck skin indicated she was perilously dehydrated and needed water as an electrolyte solution. It turns out she needed several five-liter jugs of electrolyte fluid intravenously before even trying to pump water into her rumen to give her the amount of fluid she needed to survive.

The containers of electrolyte solution weighed eleven pounds each. It felt like they weighed a lot more on the way back from the truck and through the cotton field. It took an hour to give ten liters of an electrolyte solution. My patient responded very well to the fluid infusion, and the cow's skin wasn't stiff anymore. She still had to have plain water pumped into her rumen. She was sitting up with the rope halter loose so she could get up when she was ready.

The technique of pumping the stomach is designed to deliver fluid, in this case, water into the rumen.

The process involved inserting a one-inch diameter soft plastic stomach tube through a speculum placed in the mouth of the cow. The tube continued down the esophagus and into the rumen, a journey of four feet in this cow.

To make sure the tube was in the rumen, instead of the lungs, I blew into the tube and watched the side of the cow to see and hear the bubbles entering the rumen. The outside end of the stomach tube was attached to a pump. It took twenty gallons of water to save the cow's life.

During the several hours administering different fluids, I understood that the cow was close to death for the whole duration of the treatment. I never gave that much fluids to any animal before. My patient steadily improved, so I continued cautiously until I met my goal of the cow's ability to use her legs and get up.

With that much water in her and the electrolytes balanced, it was finally safe to believe this animal would survive. The temperature in the pen when I finished read 117 on a thermometer in the shade. I could not leave the cow until she was able to get up and stay up on her own.

The forty-minute wait was good for me too, sipping iced sun tea with lemon. After perspiring as much as I did, there was the danger of dehydrating myself. I drank a thermos of iced sun tea and went back to the truck for a couple of bottles of water. The water was warm, but that's all I had. The water was worth the effort to walk through the hot cotton field again.

The cow finally got up and soon was drinking from the cattle tank. She drank for so long that her sides expanded. Now she was OK for me to leave. It felt like I spent the whole day at that corral. My finger stopped throbbing with pain. While at the truck, I cranked up the air conditioning and relaxed until I was able to drive.

The clock in the truck showed I slept through two hours with the engine running and the air conditioning on high.

The invoice I prepared ended up as a lot of money for a milk fever call. There were two ways the cow came close to dying and maybe two ways the vet could die in that hot corral. Water and common sense saved both our lives.

The fallout from the call found no mention of the cost of services, including the time. What was an important complaint was that the lariat stretched out by the corral belonged to the owner's son who spent his evenings team-roping with his friends. The lariat was laid out perfectly to allow kinks to straighten out, and I apparently left a big bend when the rope was twisted to make a halter. The kid was pretty mad.

The owner said it was all right. "Just buy him a new lariat and put it on my bill." He said. I said, "No, that's OK. I had a rope halter in my truck, and I simply used a handy rope to hold the cow in position." I had no idea of what value a young roper wannabee places on his tools, so it was my fault. I bought the lariat and finally understood the difference between a rope and a lariat, especially the cost.

As I grew older and wise in things cowboy, I learned the culture of the sport of team roping with its rules and off limits. These guys live and die to preserve the traditions. Sometimes it's easy for a vet to get in the way of some of those traditions.

THE PA'JARO FEEDLOT AND THEIR FAMOUS FLYING BURRO

The word "Pa'jaro" is Spanish for "bird." Indeed we are talking about a good-sized cattle feedlot, and yes, there were birds, thousands of birds, all the time. The feedlot had a maximum capacity of twenty thousand cattle but usually housed about half that number.

The location in the middle of nowhere between Gila Bend, Arizona, and the California state line had abundant availability of water and grain, making this feedlot an oasis for the birds. It was also far enough distance from neighbors who might complain about the smell. The animals were comfortable, and the owner made money — on a good day.

Billy, the owner, drove from his home in Phoenix every morning before the sun came up, more than a hundred-mile trip. The reason for the early arrival was twofold. First, this was the comfortable time of the day for man and beast, and second, every morning revealed another challenge of the day that was waiting.

As the veterinarian servicing this feedlot, my telephone regularly rang at five-thirty in the mornings they needed a vet. There was nothing routine about my work those mornings.

"Doc, can you fix a broken penis on a burro?" Billy asked. Wow! What a way to wake up. I got the particulars on what happened; how serious, and what we needed to have on my truck, and then I set off for the desert trip.

Billy's question about whether I could fix a broken penis on a burro was unanswered. The answer would be, "Don't know, never done that."

"Jack" was bigger than most burros at about five hundred pounds in my calculation to determine what and how much anesthesia was needed. Jacks and mules do not respond to the conventional anesthesia protocol for horses so that it can be tricky. It's hard to imagine what kind of damage this burro had done to himself.

The story of how this happened had to wait until we finished with the surgery. I wanted to hear the story. It would add another mule story to my repertoire.

"Jack" stood quivering in pain, so we had to address that in the cocktail for anesthesia. Another drug was used to desensitize the swollen penis and to keep it outside his prepuce so we would not have to struggle with his pulling it back in before we finished.

Penises do not break. There are no bones in the penis of equines. In this case, "Jack" did damage to a blood vessel or the spongy tissue that gets engorged with blood during an erection.

Fortunately, it was an artery that was bleeding, so that was a relief. The worst scenario was to have the blood trapped in the spongy sinus tissue. In that case, we would be doing an amputation.

During the cleaning of the penis preparing for surgery, it appeared that an abundance of "goats heads" stickers and gravel were in evidence. I absolutely wanted to hear this story now!

The lump of a blood clot was as big as my two fists, and it was on the left side of the shaft, causing the penis to deviate to the right, making it look like a broken bone. The skin was lanced, releasing blood and clots. The artery was still pumping weakly, but easy to find and to ligate, stopping the flow. I also had private access to a military anti–capillary bleeding solution that ensured no further bleeding. A little spray of Gentamicin antibiotic before closing with firmly buried stitches finished my surgery.

The drug that extended his penis was wearing off, so Billy's grandfather, an old racehorse trainer, slathered the penis with his cure-all, DMSO. It couldn't hurt, so showing respect for Grandpa's superior intelligence was a good plan, especially when it involved horses and women,

"Jack" got an intramuscular injection of a reversal drug and within three minutes he got up, his penis disappeared into his sheath, and he started looking for the mare that caused all this trouble.

Billy broke out a box of breakfast burritos (no, there isn't burro meat in breakfast burritos) and a pot of cowboy coffee and we all adjourned to a couple of hay bales to hear what happened.

Eduardo and Jose' were going to breed a Quarterhorse mare to "Jack" in hopes of getting a mule offspring for feedlot work when it grew up and trained. The problem was that the mare was a tall horse, and what "Jack" wanted, he couldn't reach.

The feedlot had all kinds of chutes, including ones that could be elevated to any height. The Vaqueros rigged up the curved chute so "Jack" could come around the bend and see the object of his desire, which was anything in "season." Eduardo held the mare at the end of the chute. Their idea was that the lady horse would stand for the burro and hope that he could gain footing on the elevated chute and mount the mare.

Well, it didn't happen that way. When "Jack" saw the mare, he bellowed a noisy braying love song that scared the dickens out of the mare. She took off. "Jack" kept coming, still honking loudly. When he hit the end of the chute, which was three feet above the ground, he launched, ready to penetrate the mare, which no longer was interested.

Jose' added while laughing, "That "Jack," he kept coming out of that chute and he was flying, man! His penis was so big! You should see the look on his face when he was up there." Jose' opened his mouth wide and made his eyes pop out to mimic the burro.

Everybody was on the ground laughing by now, and it got worse when, Eduardo, who could hardly speak English, broke in to describe how "Jack" hit the ground. I got the gist of his story. Evidently "Jack" was flying with all four feet spread out, his ears were like airplane wings, and his landing gear was his manhood His landing gear didn't have wheels.

On the drive back to the clinic I found myself laughing a lot, re-living the early morning experience. All that and I would arrive early for my scheduled ten O'clock small animal appointments.

Two hours later Billy called and said that "Jack" kicked the door off his pen and went straight to where the mare was. He "covered" her twice without help, except maybe from me. The stitches held.

THE GIANT PLUNGER
A PA'JARO FEEDLOT EPISODE

I had only one client who called me way too early in the morning, so there was no need for an introduction. "Good morning Billy. What's going on?" I asked.

Billy said, "We have a problem here with one of the big blue silos. It started giving us fits two days ago, but this morning we can't get any silage out to feed our eighteen thousand feeder steers."

"Do you have anything else to feed until you get this fixed? I asked. How about the other silos, is the silage in them cured yet? If not, don't try feeding it." Billy replied, "We have plenty of grain to mix and several kinds of hay, mostly a grass mix." "Good. I said, Increase the grain mix only 10 percent and free feed the hay as loose hay. That won't set them back if it lasts less than two days. Don't let the feed bunkers run out of something for the steers to eat. We don't want to disrupt those microbes in the steer's rumen if possible."

The Harvestore rep was out the day before, but Billy had no confidence that the young salesperson knew anything about servicing these big blue glass and steel silos. Billy wanted me to come out and discuss the situation. "It looks like a 700-ton plug of silage going up and down, depending on the temperature," Billy said.

Billy knew I was a mechanical idiot and anything I said concerning how his equipment functioned he should forget, but my quick advice on how to feed his steers in the feedlot saved him probably at least twenty-five thousand dollars a day for the duration of this problem. My goal was to limit the adverse effects of a sudden change in diet multiplied by eighteen thousand steers.

My schedule wouldn't allow me to get to the feedlot until one or two O'clock. Our Rotary club sponsored a career day at the high school that day, and I was obligated until noon to speak about opportunities of being a veterinarian.

At the feedlot, Billy called me to give directions to the Harvestore silo that had the problem. We both used those new "brick" analog telephones of the Eighties. They were hilariously heavy, clumsy, and seemed to me that they were always hot, but they worked and weighed one-tenth as much as the two-way radios that hardly ever worked. Cell phones still were not available to the public.

Billy bought five of these big, blue silos called Harvestores. They were designed very much like a Mason "fruit jar" in that they were glass on the inside and the outside was steel. The silos were sealed from the atmosphere, just like the jars my mom used for canning peaches.

The silos were delivered and erected in February. Four months later, in June the corn and milo crops were ready to harvest. The entire plant above the ground in each case was food for the cattle, but first, the material had to go through a fermentation process that took six weeks. During that time, a variety of yeasts and bacteria changed the fresh crop of corn and milo into easier to digest starches, sugars, and amino acids. The first silo worked out as expected, but the second silo on-line had a major problem.

What troubled Billy at the moment was his investment in feeding eighteen thousand steers worth on the average of $750.00 each. He was responsible for this venture of over thirteen million dollars! The diet for cattle cannot be changed abruptly without consequence, and in Billy's situation it meant the cows stop gaining weight

For a better perspective, feeder cattle increased their weight from three to four pounds a day. In a feeding disruption like this episode, the steers not only failed to gain those pounds but also lost another four pounds. That lost weight adds up to eight pounds lost immediately and three more days added to the time in the feedlot. The Pa'jaro Feedlot had a risk of losing at least $100,000 a day that this silo was down if they couldn't feed the cattle properly. The other three silos were not adequately fermented, so the silage was not ready for three weeks.

Gila Bend had the reputation of one of the hottest spots in America. Afternoon temperatures have been recorded as high as one hundred twenty-five degrees in the shade, but the normal summer high is 110 degrees. At night in the arid desert air, the temperature sometimes dropped into the fifty's.

An air space at the top of the silage was supposed to be sealed to keep oxygen away from the silage. That air space was subject to crazy differences in atmospheric pressure, due to the temperature fluctuations in the desert. These silos had controls to stabilize the pressure. Obviously, that was the problem. Gravity pushed the forage (silage) down with reasonable force and delivered the material into machinery at the bottom. The machine at the bottom dug out the silage onto a conveyor and into the feed trucks. The feed trucks mixed in the grain, chopped hay, and a premix of vitamins and minerals. The cattle got a balanced diet every day.

Cold temperatures at night decreased the air space at the top. The temperature drop created a powerful vacuum strong enough to pull the entire content seven hundred ton plug of silage up as far as twelve feet. With no silage at the bottom, there was no feed for the cows.

During the hot day, as the air expanded, the heated air pushed down the plug of silage into the extraction machinery like a sledgehammer, and again, there was no silage coming out. At the transition between extreme pressure and vacuum, there were only ten minutes when the extraction machinery worked.

I understood what the physical problem was, but my mind got fuzzy when it involves machinery. This situation received a veterinarian's diagnosis as something was broke in the control of the air space. That's why God made engineers, and Dick, my brother-in-law, was a civil engineer. He was also the smartest man I ever met. We called him in Columbus, Ohio.

I was trying to describe the problem to Dick when he stopped me with, "You can stop now. You're confusing me. What you need to do is simple. Put your friend on the phone, so I can tell him what he needs and what to do with it".

Dick's advice must have been a pretty simple solution. Billy went into

Gila Bend (Population 675 friendly folks and seven old grumps) and came back with everything he needed to fix the problem. He had a nitrogen gas tank, one hundred feet of small bore copper tubing, a pop-off valve, and a connector that fit the port that every Harvestore silo has for just this problem. (And the Harvestore rep should have known about that.)

There was a possibility of life-threatening danger when connecting to the port. It was possible to blow off the top of the silo if a built in pop-off valve didn't work. The pressure in this case probably was over 10,000 PSI. Even just opening the port released a jet of rushing air capable of at least cutting through the skin, or even tear off an arm. Billy wisely decided to wait until three in the morning, when the pressure was stable, and he fixed the pop-off mechanism.

I drove home knowing everything would be OK, and it was. My job was to recommended how to feed the steers until the silo problem got fixed. Dick had the immediate information to solve the problem, and Billy set it within twenty hours. The Harvestore company people in nearby Buckeye probably would have fixed it quickly, but their two repair people were fishing off the coast of Mexico.

Dick and Mary helped me many more times they were aware. It is an interesting trade-off with us. Maybe Dick had backed away from that "strongest man on earth" complement by now, but back in the day when we were both students at the university I probably showed off a bit when there was a chance.

Dick stopped to visit at my apartment on the west side of Columbus. When he tried to leave, somebody with a Volkswagen "Beetle" parked behind his vintage Ford truck, leaving less that a foot between the vehicles.

We both thought that was bad manners, or at least rude. Two young men stopped to talk to Dick about his predicament. They suggested moving the Volkswagen.

We decided to pick up the Volkswagen and park it between a light post and a pillar just a few feet on the other side of the sidewalk. They thought the Beetle's owner deserved at least a free moving job. They were anxious to help.

The Volkswagen Beetle looked like a lightweight in the sixties, but they still weighed 1,735 pounds! Most of that was in the rear since the motor was there.

I grabbed the right front bumper and slid the right wheel onto the sidewalk. The other three guys thought they could handle the rear end and do the same, but they couldn't. With a fourth person joining them, the rear wheel was soon on the sidewalk. Repeating the process twice, the Beetle was snug as the bug it was named after, with only an inch to spare at the light post. The front touched the stone pillar at the entrance to an insurance agency.

The prank was good for laughs all around when we thought about what the owner's face looked like when he came back to find his car was the one that was stuck. I guess that identified all four of us as nerds.

ONE SORE HORSE
A PAJ'ARO FEEDLOT EPISODE

It was February in Arizona, and the phone rang at 5:30 in the morning, so it had to be Billy. His frequent early morning calls made me wonder if I should just get in the truck and surprise him at 5:30 in the morning. "Billy's not here yet, but we have a bad accident happen with one of my racehorses," said Max, Billy's grandfather from Morenci.

Max has been around so long that he was probably old. For sixty years or so his work with racehorses took him to so many racetracks big and small that he doesn't remember half of them. I was surprised he didn't treat this horse himself.

Max's treatment for everything was DMSO, a chemical extracted from trees. Through the years, DMSO has shown good healing and pain relief properties. It was a bit primitive, but it worked.

"I'll be on my way in ten minutes, I said, Is there anything special that you need to have?" "Yeah, bring your stuff for lockjaw and if you have some DMSO, bring me a gallon." Why is it I buy eight ounces of DMSO and it gets old on the shelf? He wants gallons!

When I arrived, Billy was there, along with all the feedlot hands. They were at the horse paddocks, and it looked like a lot of digging was going on. A beautiful bay mare was impaled on a steel fence post. The cowboys were digging around the base of the steel fence post.

Their intentions were good, but the deeper the hole around the post, the farther down the horse sank. The top of the post broke through the skin and protruded six inches above the shoulder. Max was pouring his

DMSO into the wound from above, but most of it splashed on the ground into the hole they were digging. The scene reminded me of the Keystone Kops comedy clips.

"Billy, do you have something that can cut through this steel fencepost quickly? I asked. He did have just what I hoped for, a Skill Saw with a diamond blade. "It will make a lot of noise and spook the horse," warned Max.

I was thinking the same as I concocted the precise formula to sedate the horse. The first step was injecting a local anesthetic around the wound area. That took a lot of Lidocaine and about four minutes. Next, the IV injection addressed the tranquilizer effect to take away the anxiety, followed with a second IV injection separately to minimize the deep pain. We did not want the horse to go to sleep and fall down on the post.

I wanted to give the injections early so the medications would be in effect when we removed the post. We planned on removing the post by pulling it up and through two feet of the muscle of the shoulder and chest, but first, we had to get rid of the anchor plate at the bottom of the steel fencepost.

I had all the injections in the right places when Billy came back with the saw and a long extension cord. The saw made short work cutting through the steel, and it certainly made an awful lot of noise! One of the cowboys sprayed the steel post with water to keep it cool and to diminish the hot sparks damage.

The post protruded out six inches above the shoulder and two feet below the chest. The bottom part of the post that had the anchor attached was cut off.

The structures of the mare's shoulder between those points were the muscle bundles, ligaments, fascia, nerve trunks, bone and major blood vessels. That's a lot to consider regarding possible major damage when the contaminated fencepost was being pulled through.

After a quick review of equine anatomy, it appeared the fencepost bluntly forced its way through the pectoral muscle group without much damage. I determined the scope of damage in the lower area by exploring the bottom hole with my gloved hand. From there the post traveled up through the space between the scapula and the rib cage and came out on the side of the neck in an area with mostly ligaments that would heal in time.

I clearly identified the larger blood vessels located near the bottom hole. That was the only danger zone, and I planned to protect the arteries and veins with my hand.

Once the mare experienced no pain, we had about five minutes left to remove the post before the horse would start feeling sensations again.

We sanitized both ends of the post with iodine and a thick rope of twisted gauze bandage attached on the bottom end, and we soaked the bandage with Furacin solution to kill bacteria. We probably used a hundred feet of gauze bandage.

We then pulled the post upward until we were past the blood vessels. Billy pulled it out the rest of the way while I was feeding the soaked gauze from below.

The gauze wick was pulled through until there was no more dirt on the gauze. The patient made no quick moves during this part, thank goodness. Then we stuffed as much gauze into the wound as we could to act as a drain.

Guess what we soaked the gauze with: You guessed it, DMSO. It was perfect for this injury, and it pleased Max.

Tetanus prevention shots and penicillin once daily injection instructions were left for Max to give. The aftercare for the wound was simple; Max pulled out two feet of gauze daily from each end until it was all removed. No gauze should remain in the wound. The workers were instructed to walk the horse twice a day for twenty minutes.

The outcome was perfect. I never saw the horse again. Max brought her to the ranch in Morenci where she spent the rest of her years as a broodmare.

Steel posts have no business in horse pens. They are an accident that will happen in time. In this case, the mare was playing/fighting. She reared up pawing with her front feet and came down on the top of the post. There were at least five hundred pounds of horse coming down on that jagged steel point. Ouch!

GHOSTS OF WALDEN

Driving a rental car from the Columbus Airport in late April to Walden, Ohio was a mistake; I told myself. A terrible mistake at the moment, but then, maybe this was the beginning of a pleasant change in my life.

I left Phoenix and its warm days and beautiful nights at nine O'clock PM for the "Red Eye Special," which brought me to Columbus in a little over three hours. Add three more hours for time difference and my arrival time was three in the morning.

Sleeping on a plane never agreed with me. Checking into a hotel and catch up on some sleep would have been the sensible thing to do, but I didn't do it.

A heavy snowfall hit the Interstate 40 east of Columbus in the area called the Hocking Hills. It would be pretty in the daylight I thought. Then, Whoa! A deer bounded across the highway not fifty feet in front of the car. She was the first of a total of eight deer sightings on this 100-mile trip. I thought maybe my Guardian Angel directed those deer to wake up drowsy motorists like me. It was effective, for sure!

After a lot of discussion with Zandy and the same amount of research, we decided to come back to Ohio after fourteen years in Arizona. She was born in Southeastern Ohio, and we both loved the place. The Ohio Valley was "home" to her and she felt better with her lupus in Ohio's climate. The question was, "Could we make a decent living in Appalachia on just my income?"

At the turn-off south from the Interstate 40, the first thing I noticed was that the lesser state and county highways had no snow removal like the Interstate did.

I had it right; the snow was beautiful, all eight inches of it. Under the snow was a green countryside, shocked by a very late winter weather system.

I still had thirty miles to go over a very curvy road, so I stopped for breakfast and hoped the snowplows cleared the roads soon.

Ohio State Highway 800 from the interstate, continued south to a community named Fly on the Ohio River. It was one of the most beautiful roads in America. With the snow, it was probably the most dangerous road in America, but still beautiful. It was so full of curves that a stretch of straight road lovingly was named, the "Half-Mile Straightaway." There was not another straight stretch of road for forty miles!

After breakfast in a small town café, I felt better. Who wouldn't feel better after a country breakfast topped off with a piece of apple pie?

It was nearly seven o'clock and the end of my journey; the town of Walden showed signs of waking up as I entered what might be my new home.

A morning fog filled the dips in the scenery, with wisps trailing across a cemetery. Oh my, God, That's creepy! That was my first impression of Walden, and it gave me Goosebumps.

I was too tired to wander around the town of Walden for a place to stay for the next five days. Asking about hotels was another experience. There were no hotels or motel signs along the road coming into town, so the first step was to ask for directions. The lady I asked said that she would not stay in any of the hotels in town, but recommended a lovely bed and breakfast.

The accommodation of the bed and breakfast cottage the lady suggested was so comfortable that I decided to sleep until tomorrow. Not only was the long night with no sleep working on me, the day before was a long day also, working on a ranch near Gila Bend in the Arizona sunshine. That vet call was my last thought before I fell into a deep sleep.

I woke up in the early evening to a disturbing dream that a ghost was watching me. The hunger in my stomach was a more likely reason to wake me. The snow that fell the night before was completely gone, so I guess I slept through a beautiful spring day.

The air was clean and fresh; the part of living in Ohio that I remembered and cherished while residing in the desert for the last fourteen years.

That evening I had dinner at the Seneca Restaurant and Bar. Striking up a conversation with a stranger in town was easy. It wasn't that visitors seldom visit the village; the people were just plain curious and engaging a stranger gave lots of fuel to start an avalanche of gossip, just like Fort Recovery 200 miles west of Walden. The home cooked chicken dinner with dessert was great.

A group of three couples stopped by my table and struck up a conversation. One young man, a schoolteacher with a guitar, asked if I minded having company. After introducing who I was and what I came for, three more patrons brought their chairs to my table. In an hour they told me more about Walden than a week of research could.

The building across the street was a perfect place to renovate into a vet clinic on the street level, and I could live upstairs. Mrs. Smith lived there until she died recently of a heart attack. She was eighty-something and was a beloved old grandmother to many in the town.

At this point, one of the women mentioned that the house was home to a ghost. That started a lot of chatter. The two-story building was built before 1900, and had been a dentist's office originally and served as a funeral home, chick hatchery, library, and a residence for a few more people, last being Mrs. Smith. The family had it for sale, cheap.

The group was unanimous in the opinion that if Mrs. Smith were the ghost, none would worry about it since Mrs. Smith was the most generous and loved person in town.

Something in the manner of reinforcing that Mrs. Smith would be a friendly ghost didn't seem right; like there was a lot more not mentioned. The ghost in my dream an hour ago that woke me up looked like an ugly man.

One of the men, Perry, was a realtor and suggested that we meet for breakfast in the morning, but not too early. Perry said that the keys to that property were at his office. He suggested meeting him in the morning to show the property as well as going over specs on other properties available.

That was a lot to sleep on, but nodding off into a deep sleep was no challenge. I felt very optimistic that a move to Walden would be a test of our ability as a family to grow and provide service to a community that had no veterinarian. Thinking of fulfilling that task was an exciting challenge.

Our family should be a valuable addition to the town of 3200 people and the county, in general, I told myself. The idea of becoming wealthy in Appalachia was an oxymoron. There were no scary dreams that night. I slept ten more hours.

The next morning promised one of the most beautiful days of my life. It was as if Mother Nature gave Walden another beautiful snowfall just for me since I missed the one yesterday.

I met Perry and his wife Cindy, partners in the real estate business. We had breakfast and listened to their plans for the day. Cindy said, "After what Perry told me last night I can tell you that the town needs your family and we will do all we can to introduce you to all the possibilities of the area."

Cindy was anxious to show the house of a family friend first. She explained that there was no intention of selling the house to me, but it was a beloved property that meant a lot to her. It was an example of a quality home for a good price. She wanted to show that there were some great homes in Walden. She certainly delivered on that explanation.

Cindy grew up with a friend in that house and she just wanted to see it again before it sold. There was no need to apologize. The property was stunning with a six-inch new snowfall and a warm, bright morning sun that would surely melt all the snow in a few hours.

By the time we looked at several houses the snow had melted. Perry picked up the key for the house across the street from the Seneca and met Cindy and me at the building. I was intrigued by the prospects of an idea that was offered last night after dinner. Living above the clinic part until my family moved to Ohio fit my time line.

Zandy had a teaching contract for the rest of the school year in Arizona, and we were hoping for her to support the family in Arizona until I had a practice set up in Ohio.

The long distance would be good for me. Zandy was still mad at me because the failed embryo transplant business cost us so much money while the actual culprit appeared to get away with grand theft. I had to prove myself in her mind and regain confidence in mine.

We had lunch and Perry invited a contractor to join us and talk about renovating the building into a vet clinic for small animals. Max, the contractor, was young, husky, and talented. His resume wasn't long, but the jobs he worked on and finished showed he had confidence in his abilities.

I liked Max from the first minute. He turned out to be a diamond in the rough by the time the project finished in half the time of his estimate, and the cost was under the estimate as well.

My decision was made to go back to Arizona in three more days to prepare for going ahead on the move to Walden.

The next afternoon I visited a farmer in Lee Township for some advice. Bill was Zandy's cousin, and I wanted to get Bill and Sarah's feedback on this venture. Their dairy farm wasn't large, but it was enough to put two sons through college. The community of farmers in Berg County respected Bill, and I had asked him before I made this trip what he and his wife thought about a middle-aged veterinarian trying to start a practice in the area.

He was an earnest and thoughtful man and had some advice for me. First, he was solidly for having a few more family settling in the county. Personally, he lived in an area that was poorly serviced by veterinarians, so he gave me his blessings to the venture.

We talked about his cousin, Zandy, her teaching job, her disease and our marriage. His advice was to move her to Walden as soon as possible. He said, "It would be good for her lupus but don't make her stay in that haunted house when she gets here, or she will leave." He had the name of a rheumatologist in Wheeling that would be happy to include her in his clientele.

"How did you know about the supposedly haunted house?" I asked. "Max is "Linc's" best motorcycle buddy, and I just got off the phone with my son, Lincoln. Did you visit him yet?" he asked. "Not yet, but I will before I leave on Friday" I answered. Linc was the prosecuting attorney for Berg County.

I brought the conversation back to the haunted house and that I wondered if it would be a problem. His answer was that a ghost wouldn't hurt anybody, but it can mess with your head if you let it. "Remember, you are your best friend or your worst enemy. Continue being a solid moral person and you can overcome anything, even ghosts."

That was a strange piece of advice. I wondered if Bill knew something I didn't know about that house. One thing was evident; this man believed there was a ghost in that house.

The remaining time was spent driving through the county. What a trip! This county had so much beauty and industry. Much of the population descended from Swiss miners in the coalfields a century ago.

A young national forest in the making included one-fourth of the county. The Forest Service was buying all the small and abandoned farms available for what seemed to be for a fair price. In a hundred years the Wayne National Forest will be a showpiece of forest management.

Coal mining was another story. A century ago, more than five thousand men worked in the mines. In the 1980's two hundred employees including the clerical staff produced twice as much more coal by deep wall mining, but this process fractured the underground strata, causing water retention and quality of groundwater problems. Abundant natural resources seem to lead to copious social and water problems.

The entire county was hilly. If the hills were flattened somehow, the area would probably cover the State of Maryland. The hills were the beauty of Berg County.

I drove through the county for two days and probably saw less than one percent of the land, and the land I saw was spectacular! Every bend in the road revealed something interesting. I loved the area and vowed to come back. As time passed, I did come back in two weeks with my pickup truck packed with a lot of veterinary stuff and not much else.

Max started revamping the first floor to accommodate an X-ray machine, surgery room, and an exam room. The reception room was the small sitting room with an antique gas fireplace to match a rather old portrait of Lincoln. The upstairs was livable as it was. The kitchen upstairs was a cozy place to have a Laz Y Boy reading chair, so I was content. Even though I was able to cook for myself, it was so much more convenient, cheaper, and healthier to eat across the street at the Seneca. I was settled in upstairs immediately, and Max finished the remodeling in less than four weeks.

My first month in Walden was spent introducing myself to prospective customers both for large animal and for pets. The Board of Health had an advertisement for someone to fill the position of Health Commissioner, so I looked into that as well. There wasn't much I could do to help Max with his construction.

The most costly item for the vet clinic was a beautiful hand painted sign indicating the doctor was in. It was a bit big for where we wanted it hung, so naturally, when the first storm blew through the town, one chain broke loose, and the swinging sign shattered the nearby window.

The window was nine feet tall and difficult to replace locally. A plywood sheet covered the broken window for two weeks until a new window replaced it. Add that cost to what I paid for the sign, and I probably had the most valuable sign in town. That was the second time I thought about the ghost.

All old houses have stairs that squeak and things that go "bump" in the dark. Sometimes I would turn on the lights and investigate to satisfy myself that it was nothing, and it was always nothing out of the ordinary.

One day I came across something that was not ordinary. I noticed that the gas company bill was the same every month. It was not a big bill for the summertime, but especially when the weather turned cold, it was still $6.75 a month. I walked to the gas company three blocks up the hill to mention it. The meter reader man said that it was OK, "Nobody wants to read your meter, and so we leave it alone. That bill has been that amount ever since I worked at the gas company". He was with the gas company twenty years, reading meters!

"That house has a bad ghost from what I hear," he said. He declined an invitation to take a look at the meter. I was secretly hoping for some company so I wouldn't be going into the cellar alone. I realized that I never visited the cellar since I moved in.

What I discovered in the basement was a rusted gas line that still delivered gas with no gassy smell. That was good. The meter was in the fruit cellar along with two sets of shelves that stored canned goods. There were a few recently made jams and peaches, but ten times more old jars with black stuff in them.

I picked up one of those old jars and noticed how cold it was down there. It felt thirty degrees colder in the fruit cellar than the outside temperature reading in the high seventies!

An old floor type gas furnace heated the room directly above. That room now was my reception room, and that was the floor furnace that old Mrs. Smith tripped over, spilling a container of water into the heated coils, and turning the water into scalding hot steam. That was also the place they found her dead from a heart attack following the savage burns. With that, I backed out and probably ran up the basement steps; I don't remember.

I lived in that house for two years, and that was the only time I went into the fruit cellar. Now I felt for sure the house had a ghost keeping me company day and night. I remembered Bill Reithmiller's advice about being of strong moral convictions. I tried harder to believe what Bill said.

I showed the canned food jar to Greg next door to the County Health Commissioner's Office. Greg was my receptionist's husband and somewhat an antique buff. (I got the job as part-time Health Commissioner.)

"Where did you get that, and what is the black stuff in it? He asked. This piece is a really old type of jar to preserve food. It dates to before the Ball Jar Company changed its look in 1884. The patent date on the jar was 1853, so it was at least a hundred years old".

The corroded zinc lid allowed air to get into whatever was in the old glass jar. The black stuff was about a half cup of dust that maybe once was applesauce.

"Where did you find this?" he asked again. The basement experience of an hour ago was related in detail, resulting in a strange look of revelation and fear in Greg's face at the same time.

"What's wrong?" I asked. Greg then told me about an adventure he had when he was ten years old. "That building you are in is haunted. Every kid in town tried to get up enough courage to go down in the basement where they say a giant ghost lived or died. I know of only one boy that made that attempt to break into the cellar door, go down the steps and to the gas meter and touch it before he ran away. That boy was me," he said, trembling a bit. He stated that he saw jars like this one on the shelves fifteen years ago. "By the way, he added, It was very cold in the cellar." "Deena told me that she hadn't seen any sign of a ghost in your office. If she did, you would know it; she wouldn't show up as your secretary again, ever!" He said.

Greg told me he thinks the thing is harmless, but also that it does not like children.

Nothing happened. This scare was my imagination, and it will not occur again. I was inclined to believe Mrs. Smith's spirit might be roaming around, and I would be OK with that from the high regard the people in town had for her.

My son, John did visit the basement. Nobody told John anything about a haunted house. At twenty, he was no angel; his involvement with drugs interfered with his ambition to get a college degree in agriculture at his dad's Alma Mater. The Wooster, Ohio Agricultural Campus of The Ohio State University accepted John as a horticulture student.

He brought his baggage with him in the manner of bringing his girlfriend (also a drug user) and her little boy (not his). They drove to Ohio early to stay with me for a few days before enrolling at the college in Wooster two hours north of Walden. I had to leave for two days shortly after they arrived, so they were alone in a possible haunted house.

John called me into his second night at the house. His voice filled with panic, "Dad, Could you send enough money for us to stay at a motel in Wooster until I get a part time job and start classes? I'm getting out of here right now!"

"Are you in trouble?" I asked. "Oh hell yes, but not with the law. In fact, your friend the sheriff gave me a hundred dollar bill and told me to get away from that house and behave myself."

Whatever scared John was a good thing. He got enough credits for an Associates Degree in horticulture and worked two jobs during that time, paying his own college expenses. Then he spun out of control again.

More than a year passed. Reading a good book was my passion. It was not unusual for me to read the entire book in one sitting (with a few breaks), no matter how many pages it had.

This particular February night was cold and windy outside. Inside the upstairs kitchen was cozy with my cushy chair and a vented gas heater. The book had seven hundred pages, so it would be a long night unless it wouldn't be a good read.

Eight hours and a pot of coffee later, the end of the book was near. A loud crash sounded at the kitchen window. Apparently, something caused the old window to slam upward into the top of the sill, breaking the glass into hundreds of little pieces. There were no answers, but plenty questions of why the window broke like that.

Examining the window revealed that this was an old style window with weights attached to a rope inside the window frame and over a pulley. The cord was rotten and frayed, not connected to the window at all, and hadn't been for a long time!

"OK Mrs. Smith, this has gone too far! I shouted thinly through my goose bumps and terror. We're going to have Father Joe come over here and have the house exorcised. It's time for you to go home to Heaven!"

The last part about going home to Heaven I delivered in a visceral bellow that rattled the other window.

When I looked at the glass on the floor for the second time, the glass shards were all in a pile. There was no glass anywhere but in the middle of the floor! I called Greg. It was seven O'clock in the morning. "If you are my friend, come over and see what my ghost has done. You won't believe it!" I said.

When Greg. Arrived he found me in the truck with the heater on, waiting for him. I needed to be with someone other than old Mrs. Smith's spirit who let her anger scare me into stop reading that book all night. When I showed him the glass on the floor and the window, he said, "You are kidding me, aren't you?" "Serious enough to ask a priest to come over and perform an exorcism," I answered.

Greg could not find a splinter of glass anywhere else in the kitchen either. We used a powerful flashlight and still couldn't find any glass except for the pile on the floor.

The window was a puzzle. It was a good thing that this window had a storm window outside or we would freeze to death. The inside window was intact last summer when I tried to open those windows to let some air into the upstairs and at that time, I could not budge the inside window and gave up.

I called Father Joe to ask about the exorcism of spirits in a house. He didn't ask any questions. He just said, "I'll be over as soon as I can."

He came right after Greg left and told me not to say a single word, but to remain in the truck. Father Joe quickly disappeared into the house.

It seemed like Father Joe was inside the house for only a minute when he came outside and called me to come into the house with him. He looked like a different man. His face was red; his eyes were red, and he was wet with perspiration, even with the outside temperature somewhere between zero and ten degrees above zero.

"There wasn't one ghost in the house, he said. There were two spirits. One was an old woman, and the other was a man. I don't know if I did any good because I blacked out. That never happened to me before. The man was pure anger all I can say. I am sorry I couldn't help you, but there is hope. When I woke up, both spirits were gone." He explained.

When I told him he was in the house for less than a minute, he seemed relieved and said, "Maybe it did work, the exorcism. Time stands still they say." I would like to know more about "Father Joe." There was a lot more to him than just being assigned to a poor Appalachian mission in the next county and celebrating Mass in various local established parishes.

My first clue to this was when he answered my query about which Society of the priesthood he belonged. He explained that he was Italian and became a citizen of the world through his years of training in Rome as a Jesuit Priest.

He was sent to many locations to minister communities having problems with "The dark side of spirituality." I don't know for sure, but the way he blustered into a haunted house with the confidence in his ability to dispel lost spirits makes him a master exorcist in my mind. A week later he was saying his goodbyes to a small number of people offering their gratitude. None mentioned what it was that they were thankful. Neither did I.

Thanks to "Father Joe," there is an end to this ghost tale, but there is an epilog. Five years later the old house was somewhat remodeled. In the demolition of the front porch, the workers came across a grisly scene.

Under the old slab of concrete was a space called a "half-cellar" that was next to the fruit cellar room with the gas meter mentioned earlier. In that space were the bones of a giant of a man who at one time measured over seven feet tall.

A newspaper in Walden named "The Spirit of Democracy" whose own epitaph reads 1844 – 1994, carried a story that shed light on who the ghost might have been. An edition dated December 9, 1909, news clip tells of the disappearance of Big John Wyscznsky, "the town character." "Big John" was an East European immigrant who came to Berg County to work in the coalmines.

The ballads by Tennessee Ernie Ford's "Sixteen Tons," and "Big Bad John" by Jimmy Dean, pretty much described the situation with John

Wyscznsky (and many more miner heroes with the same story). In a mine explosion, Big John jammed a thick timber under a crumbling roof long enough for the trapped crew to escape to safety.

Big John survived with horrible wounds to the left side of his face, and his left arm dangled uselessly after the accident. He was a hero, and he was treated as such, except there was no compensation other than handouts and donations, mostly alcohol.

The children were the cruelest by their taunting him and throwing rocks. Evidently, "Big John" left the saloon on a cold December 9th night, 1909. The newspaper recorded a low temperature overnight five degrees below zero! Looking for a place to sleep, the half cellar was his last resting place. His spirit remained to watch over his remains for the last eighty years.

There are too many (anecdotal mostly) parts of this story to deny the presence of ghosts among the living. Now I would tell Mr. Feckler back in Indiana that indeed, I do believe in ghosts.

Belief in anything as weird as ghosts is built up slowly through experiences starting early in life. For me, I was sensitive to something like an energy source in the country cemetery just down the road from our farmhouse. I felt the coldness as I passed on my way to the mailbox pedaling my bicycle as fast as I could to get away from the place.

If you have read my stories about Fort Recovery, there are hints of violent death on a more frequent basis than most places. Berg County had that history as well; otherwise, Father Joe wouldn't have shown up.

Back to what happened to my son John that scared him; five years after his mom had died and he was counting his sober days as months, then years, we resumed our relationship.

On a desert overnight camping trip, he asked me, "Did you know that house in Walden was haunted?" "Yes, I answered. At the time I thought it was the ghost of nice Mrs., Smith. She was a friendly ghost, if anything."

He shivered in his coat, saying, "That was no Mrs. Anybody! I saw the thing. He was tall as the ceiling; his face was horrible and his left arm flopped when he moved!"

He went on to tell me about when little Billy was playing with his toy cars; the toys went flying up to the top of the window curtain rod. He didn't see a ghost, but that spooked him. He packed to leave the next morning.

He couldn't wait that long to leave as it turned out. He said that as the three were sleeping in the bed, the noisy ghost's breathing woke him and the shape of a man came over to his face breathing heavily. John could not breathe. He thought he was dying. Them Billy stirred, the ghost stood up and strode towards the closet before disappearing through the closed door.

"That's when we bailed, he said. We didn't have enough money to get to Wooster and didn't know what to do so we went to the sheriff's office and met your friend, Tink who gave us a hundred dollar bill and told me to leave that house and behave myself".

I have pictures of Walden; among them is a shot of the clinic with one of the tall windows that didn't get smashed with the sign. When John sees that picture, he blanches and catches his breath, saying. 'There he is! See that ugly face. He's tall. Can't you see it?" No, I never saw what he did. Then again, the ghost never scared me to death or hurt me in any way except maybe dropping my body temperature thirty degrees!

On cold nights during those spells where days passed without the sun shining through the clouds, and my vitamin D ran out, I fought a depressed, feeling that something was wrong with my world. I felt the muscles tightening, and I imagined my body was shriveling slowly but surely. Then the chills came in waves that heat and extra covers barely made a dent in my discomfort.

That fruit cellar image floods my imagination. Every detail of the gas meter and shelves of old fruit jars, the dank smell of something hoary, and the absolute silence pushes all other thoughts or dreams aside. There is an energy infusion felt that is alien and unwelcome.

For nearly thirty years my remedy has worked on "the spooks." I get up, stretch, and make myself a large cup of hot chocolate. Sometimes a cup of hot tea with a generous shot of Tennessee whiskey, sugar and cream will do the trick. The sun always comes up the next morning to balance the world again.

The house is now a beauty salon. The ghost is no longer there from what I hear, but I doubt it. I believe the energy is still there.

80-YEAR-OLD SAWDUST PILE

During the early years of the 20th Century, coal was the largest industry in Berg County. Wood supplied the hardwood beams for the hundreds of miles of coal mine tunnels and of course, building houses and barns made lumbering the second largest industry.

The Ohio River barges carried millions of logs down river for a thousand miles. Abundant rainfall allowed trees to grow rapidly, so the territory never ran out of timber.

Today the oaks, ash and walnut trees are selectively harvested for international exportation for furniture manufacturing around the world. Lumbering is a much smaller industry today.

One family operated a lumber mill on the same property for more than eighty years without bureaucratic harassment by the government (Environmental Protection Agency). One day, the EPA notified the Hanley family that they had a problem of epic proportions.

Jim Hanley came to the health department looking for help. The EPA was seeking penalty payment of thirteen million dollars.

He stopped first at the courthouse looking for someone who could tell him what this was all about, but he found no help.

One of his brothers and a good friend met Jim at the Seneca Bar and Grill to talk about this bombshell. The bartender suggested to Jim the Health Department seemed to be where he should go because the letter described health issues several times. Jim decided to walk to empty his head. No, he didn't have a morning drink: the bartender served the best coffee in town. Jim walked past the busy welfare department, past the courthouse again and headed up the hill to the health department. Fortunately for him, we could help.

His summons had five short paragraphs starting with "Whereas" and one beginning with, "Therefore." That line came to the point. The EPA wanted immediate payment of $13,000,000.00 in restitution for damages to the environment and health dangers caused by his business. His pile of sawdust accumulated over eighty years was in the process of being designated a Superfund Site.

That was news to everyone except for a close group of pesky citizens who filed complaints against what they considered businesses that ruined their pristine environment. These five individuals didn't associate with any known activist group, but they had several attributes in common: they were some brilliant people. They were either retired or never had a job, they shared a passion for everything natural, and they all came from California.

I've seen the decaying sawdust pile and old rotted slabs of the outside cut of logs processed twenty years or more ago. The stuff below the crust or the top of the pile was all rotted wood waste. The thing was, the mound covered acres of the family homestead and at one location the sawdust was probably more than a hundred feet deep, filling a small but deep valley between two hills.

At the bottom of the pile, a creek flowed year round, fed by springs and supported a healthy population of small fish, frogs, and turtles. The creek was more than 500 feet from the sawdust pile at its nearest point. To me, it looked like the springs delivered clear enough cold water to develop Fairhope Creek into a natural trout stream some day.

At the meeting with Jim in my office, I had two people on my mind that had a good chance to fight the EPA suit for Jim. I suggested Jim should contact "Linc," my wife's cousin and the kind of lawyer who knew the county. We made arraignments for all of us to meet in a few days.

This problem also had the name "Billy" written all over it, and I had an idea that Billy's experience was worth exploring. I talked to Jim and Linc about this entrepreneur and what Billy could do. Jim smiled at first and then burst out laughing so hard we were concerned about his heart. He thought it was preposterous. I knew it would work.

Billy, back in Arizona, would find this idea a windfall for everybody.

Billy didn't answer his phone. I forgot about the time zone difference, and the only time of the day Billy answered his telephone was five thirty in the morning, Arizona time. Sure enough, Billy answered my eight-thirty call in the morning on the second ring.

Billy owned the Paj'aro feedlot with all those cows, making Lord knows how much manure they pooped every day. He turned that manure into compost, along with the free bedding picked up every day from three racetracks and occasional sewerage sludge from the City of the Phoenix wastewater facility. His steer manure compost fertilized thousands of lawns in preparation to planting winter grass for Phoenix lawns, parks, and gardens. He made tons of money with that side business.

Explaining to Billy the situation with Jim's old sawdust pile and the EPA, I imagined his eyes lit up at the opportunity to do battle with that organization again. Billy had suits both against and by the Bureau of Land Management, EPA, Internal Revenue or FEMA for the last fifteen years, sometimes all of them at the same time.

His philosophy was not necessarily to win a case. That would be the expensive route. Billy's only full-time lawyer on retention frustrated the legion of federal attorneys until they dropped their allegations more times than not.

The attorney, Franklin Benjamin, Esq. (Frank), collected a one million dollar retainer in his bank account on the first Monday after the New Year for his lifetime. Also, "Frank" had carte blanche access for all legal expenses. Billy loved pressure, and he had the money to make sure the pressure fell on the other party.

After all, Billy was in the waste business from its origin to the finished product. Environmental groups liked to bring suits to federal agencies against people like Billy.

"Hey, Doc, If you want me to come out to Ohio, I'll do it next week." He said. Billy recently married my daughter's best friend, and the newlyweds were so busy they didn't have a honeymoon.

"That would be great, I said. If the two of you are OK with it, I'll pay for your stay at your choice; either Oglebay Park in Wheeling or the Riverboat Resort called Lafayette on the Ohio River in Marietta, or both if it works out for you. That can be your wedding gift from us. It would be good to see Jessica and you again."

Billy promised they would be coming the next week to look around for a couple of days first before meeting our group.

I want to make one thing clear; this plan was not mine. I watched Billy forge unbelievable waste product problems into colossal business ventures. He wasn't yet thirty-five years old, but in the last fifteen years he was broke twice and wealthy three times. If anybody could beat the EPA bully in a fair fight, it would be Billy. Heck, he would beat or extremely frustrate them even with the cards stacked against him.

The newlyweds had a unique honeymoon. They did stay at Oglebay Park three days and set up agreements with two racetracks for their waste straw and hay. Two nearby cities would gladly have Billy take their waste sludge for free as opposed to their current practice of paying for landfill tipping fees to bury it. Both cities contracted for compost to use in their parks.

The clincher would be to acquire the thousands of cubic yards of sawdust, cheap. The old decomposed sawdust as the main ingredient made their compost a better and longer lasting nutrient package for gardening and landscaping.

When the meeting with Jim, "Linc," the attorney, and Billy occurred in Marietta at the riverboat resort, Jim was nervous because he thought for sure he was going to lose everything.

After the introductions, Billy said to Jim, "I want to buy all the sawdust you have on the site and whatever you produce until you decide to quit the sawmill business. The Bill of Sale will call it "in perpetuity," but it's the same thing. I will lease the land for as long as it has a sawdust supply and I would like to pay the lease in a single payment of fifty thousand dollars. Now I want to buy outright the sawdust pile for fifteen hundred dollars."

Jim just stood there, shaking, with his mouth forming a silent, "What the Hell?" His fortunes changed from dismal to glorious in a few seconds, and it was too much to sort it out all at once. We explained what Billy could do for him earlier, but evidently, he didn't believe it.

"Then what happens about the suit the EPA filed on me? How am

I going to be able to pay the Government thirteen million dollars?" Jim asked "Linc."

"I am representing your case pro bono," Linc explained to Jim. "You no longer own the waste, once you sign the contract." Linc continued, "The EPA people are not concerned about it anymore because now it isn't waste. It's product and an essential element of compost. We politely asked the EPA to drop the suit, and they agreed."

Jim had to sit down. Things were going too fast for him, but it at least was going in the right direction.

The ripple effect was that the other three of the "Product" sources the EPA had filed lawsuits against were also dropped. The three other lawsuits involved two municipal sewage treatment facilities and a large racetrack. A second racetrack did not have a lawsuit against them yet, and their waste was coming to the Berg County compost operation instead of hauling their waste to the regional landfill.

Linc wasted no time clearing the legal issues for these four clients he represented. For them, it meant they delivered their waste with no tipping fee of twenty-five dollars a ton, and for Billy, he had thousands of tons of compost ingredients coming in for a one-time investment of fifty-one thousand five hundred dollars.

Best of all, the environmental activists thought this was an excellent idea of their thinking.

Billy managed the compost business from Phoenix. The compost manufacturing yard was ten miles from the Ohio River. The finished product went to a bagging facility next door to a river barge loading station. Soon he was moving compost up and down the Ohio River by barges to two major large cities. Eighteen months later he sold the business for eleven million dollars clear, to an entrepreneur from the East Coast.

Jim sold his sawmill to the new composter owner and started another lumber business in West Virginia. He's still a local "good 'old boy." West Virginia is only 16 miles away, across the Ohio River. Jim's fortunes kept coming. The land he bought near Sistersville, West Virginia now has a dozen natural gas wells, together pushing out a million dollars a month.

Ironically, the EPA ended up with the biggest windfall. A federal regional landfall in the next county was to be the recipient of all the sawdust according to their plan. Hauling that amount of sawdust alone would cost the government millions. The fines were supposed to pay for that and more to build another regional landfill since the sawdust was estimated to be enough to fill one and a half landfills.

Now, without the sawdust, horse manure, and sludge overflowing the landfill problem, there was enough capacity to service five counties for twenty-five more years as a regional landfill. It took a country lawyer and a manure merchant to school the EPA and made it seem like it was their idea.

BOX S RANCH

The Gallougher boys were hard to miss wherever they went in the hill country of Southeastern Ohio. They were cowboys, after all. Ever since their parents introduced them as youngsters to the grand open spaces of Colorado, Idaho, California and Arizona on a road trip to Disneyland, they were "cowboys".

They were so excited about being in the Western cowboy country that the stay in Pasadena for Disneyland had to be cut short for lack of enthusiasm.

The whole family made good use of the extra days (and money) by taking side trips into the real West, like the World's Oldest Rodeo in Prescott and the Grand Canyon in Arizona.

At a Hereford ranch in Westcliffe, Colorado, their host talked the family into staying several days for trout fishing and discussing lots of "cow business".

The boys had a good grandparents experience. Their home was a second house on the family farm so working cattle with Grandpa and 4-H activities, along with school, filled their days.

High school sports and team opportunities were not offered due to the small enrollment of the school. The American Legion organized summer baseball and softball games that the boys and girls engaged in, but the Gallougher boys had another sport of sorts. Horseback riding and working cattle came naturally. Jackpot calf team roping was their strong suit when it came to competitive sports.

Cows were the family business of the Galloughers. Their grandfather started as an operator of mammoth earth moving equipment for the coal strip-mining business, the only job available in the area.

When the war called for recruits to fight for their country, he answered and joined the Army Engineers, building landing fields all over the world.

After the war he returned to the Southeastern Ohio countryside he loved. Instead of going back to working in the coalfields he bought a farm with a veterans loan and raised beef cows. A local meat processing plant bought all the two-year-old grass fed steers. The best heifers were added to the growing herd.

In time, the meat processing business changed from small butcher shops to large companies capable of processing a thousand animals a day. That was when the Galloughers changed to selling calves weaned at about ten months of age and hauled off to farmers or feedlots where they were fed for a year before selling them to the large meat packing companies. Within a few years those in the feedlot business grew in size to feedlots with thousands of feeder cattle.

Ben Gallougher, the boys' father grew up in the cattle business. He built a house on the property and raised his family the same way except his boys were expected to earn college degrees.

Ron and Jon earned their degrees at the Agricultural College at Wooster, and Matt graduated in beef management at the state university with a masters' degree. Matt's Master's degree paper was, "Beef Management for Profit on Marginal Lands". That report became Matt's guide as a work in progress for many years.

Ben Galloughers family raised six hundred breeding beef cows, producing feeder calves in the fall for finishing at various feedlots in the tri-state area of Ohio, Pennsylvania, and West Virginia.

The seasons started with calving during the middle of winter and extended through March. Daily feeding of hay from the last year's haymaking effort was a continuous chore, as was helping the momma cows with delivering their calves when it was necessary.

Sometimes a veterinarian's assistance was called for. I was not their vet. Their farm was forty miles north of my practice area in Walden, but I met the young men at a few county fairs and at the western store operated by Marcus Weisshut and his family.

The discussion at every meeting with them that I recall was always centered on rangeland management. Everybody else in Ohio called it "pasture management".

Ron and Jon were twins and Matt made the three look like triplets. Hard work sculpted their bodies with wide muscular shoulders and years of riding horses gave them a bit of bowed legs to go with their cowboy boots and Stetsons. All three brothers bought into the cowboy dream and loved the work on the farm. To them it was a ranch.

Their mother died from cancer in 1969 and was robbed of the pleasures of watching her boys grow into fine young men. Their dad was the manager of the cattle enterprise, so as the boys grew, so did the size of the herd.

Matt just received his Master's Degree in beef cow management and returned to the family business. Jon was a part-time volunteer fireman and Ron worked also as an EMT part time. Their work on the farm was full time.

When I met them in 1987, all three were finished with their education and were living at home with their father. The energy and ambition of the boys grew into a plan to expand the herd to more than two thousand breeding cows.

On one of their many visits to the Weisshut family western clothing store, Marcus Weisshut told the brothers that Dr. Tebbe had more than a little contact with Arizona ranchers successfully grazing large expanses of land.

That was stretching the truth, but I did admire what Allan Savory was trying to do. I was one of his fans.

Matt was very interested in the method of grazing cattle on marginal land called the Savory Method but he had no experience of the method. The controversial method was causing excitement, pro and con on Allan Savory's holistic approach to halt the desertification of what he termed the "brittle environment" around the world.

Five years earlier I attended a seminar at the University of Arizona with Allan Savory as the guest professor along with a rancher from Northeast Arizona who was practicing the method for about three years.

The Ranch manager was impressed with early results but admitted at that time there was, "A bloody lot more to learn".

That seminar was mostly theory and short on specifics. It was spellbinding. Allan Savory never repeated himself in his presentation. The man was, and still is a genius. I have been reading about the Savory grazing management system ever since. His theories are regarded as the spear tip of a paradigm shift in managing animal grazing in difficult terrain.

The conditions for managing a cow-calf operation on leased land, as the Galloughers envisioned were favorable in that the Wayne National Forest had considerable acreage available to lease for grazing. The Forest Service was also a source of information concerning abandoned farms that were privately owned and were available for grazing.

One of the concerns of the forest service was the accumulation of dried grass and weeds on these abandoned small farms. The dry grass and weeds outside the jurisdiction of the forest service were a fire hazard that they had no control of.

The abandoned farms were scattered throughout the stands of forest hardwoods and pine trees. The Forest Service approved the idea of grazing those abandoned farms by local enterprises like the Galloughers because grazing National Forest Lands was always a part of their management plan. The idea of the Savory method and its benefits was hoped to become an important tool.

At the time I was living in Berg County there were more than four hundred abandoned farms in the county, owned by previous residents but now fallen in disrepair for many years. Meadows still had surviving grasses and legumes from the days when small herds grazed and hay was harvested.

Trees were making their presence as the forest began the slow process of filling in these abandoned farms with saplings. In forty years the forest would be continuous and in forty more years, timber could be harvested. A robust deer population claimed the land as their own in the meantime.

The Savory system of grazing was expected to help make the forest healthier. The holistic properties to the land from managed grazing marginal land had proven to enhance land fertility and the ability to retain rainfall, all over the world.

The difference between the Savory method and conventional grazing was, in the Savory plan, the cattle grazed very much like ancestral cattle and today's African game animals. The animals ate until half the biomass growing on a pasture was either consumed or trampled into the ground. At that time, the herd moved to another nearby "cell", leaving the previous pasture time to refresh.

With a larger herd grazing the location in a short time frame, the land benefited from a heavy dose of cow manure and urine, along with trampled grass and other vegetation. The time to heal the land after intense grazing was important.

Successful programs reported that after a pasture grazed by the Savory method area was rested for a period of time and revisited when the land was refreshed, the next grazing period presented a more lush growth of grasses than the previous use That period was anywhere from six months to five years.

The advantages of such a grazing method were many; including being profitable, but nothing was both easy and profitable when it comes to handling cows. The grazed land received the benefits as more fertility in the soil, less erosion, better water retention, and in many countries, it meant the difference between desert and savanna.

Knowledge of the land grazed was essential. There were areas in the Wayne National Forest located over active coal mining operations that fractured the ground strata when the deep wall mining process removed coal a thousand feet below. This technology disrupted the water table and caused the ground water to disappear at the surface.

Cows drink a lot of water. If there was no well to produce it, ponds were constructed to collect precipitation. The water problem in Southeastern Ohio is not precipitation. An average of forty inches of rainfall and snow fell on the land every year since forever, but keeping it in the soil was a problem.

The pond bottoms were sealed to prevent leakage into the fractured soil strata above the coal mining effects. Fenced ponds still provided drinking water for cows by connecting water tanks to the ponds by pipes. Keeping cows out of wet streambeds and ponds areas helped to reduce parasites. In addition, cows like clean water too.

The energy of the Gallougher family and the education Matt received guaranteed that the project would be attacked with scientific thinking and good old fashioned, common sense. The jump from running a cow-calf operation of 600 animal units (1 cow and her calf) to two thousand units was a challenge, but the ultimate goal was to handle three times that many animals. They realized the first years would be a learning curve. I suggested they consider ten years would be more realistic.

They received another resource with the Ohio State University Bull Evaluation Station, also in Nelsonville where they decided to introduce Salers bulls' genetics into their breeding program. They chose heifers from that cross breeding as replacements and additions to grow the herd.

The Salers breed is an old Basque breed of hardy cows with superior calving ease, excellent milk production and excellent mothering characteristics. It is estimated the breed is as old as 10,000 years. The tight genetics delivered fruits of natural selection for many generations in the Gallougher herd.

I told the Galloughers about a beef carcass study in Arizona at the Paj'aro feedlot where thirty first generation crossbred Salers carcasses were compared to thirty Angus/Hereford cross carcasses. The Salers carcasses were smaller than the Hereford/Angus carcasses, but they were in the feedlot four months less than the Hereford/Angus (called "black baldys") and the Salers cross were "finished" earlier, meaning the proportion of lean meat and choice cuts were better marbled.

"Marbled" is a term that defines the way fat is distributed in the lean meat, making a better taste and healthier digestion of fat in the steaks and roasts.

The size of the loin cut of the Salers cross was ten percent larger than the older and bigger Hereford/Angus cross. Those data meant the Salers calves were worth more per pound at weaning time. These Salers calves became the product of the Gallougher "Ranch" for years.

Before I left Berg County I stopped at the Galloughers to leave them a present of a branding iron. A fellow Rotarian in Litchfield Park, Arizona gave me the ownership of the branding rights to the Box S in Arizona. More cattle in Arizona had that brand than any other. It belonged to the Swift Meatpacking Company

I left Berg County before this plan really took off, so we lost how the operation fared. The internet calf auctions did indicate that the Gallougher Ranch calves sold for top dollar and the numbers sold rose to over two thousand calves a year.

I would like to finish this story with a suitable ending, but my suspicion is that these people turned out very well in all respects. When I call my friends from Walden, asking how the Gallougher boys are doing, I get, "They're doing great; drive big Dodge pickups and dominate the feeder calf auctions in Southeastern Ohio."

Small Calves at Birth and good Mothering Instincts
Freestock Photo Google

PAIN IN THE NECK

What was I doing in Southeastern Ohio? The short story is that the Ohio Valley was dear to my wife, Zandy. During our fifteen years in Arizona, we visited our relatives in Southeastern Ohio annually; It was Zandy's home base. Our life in Arizona just made some radical changes concerning Zandy's lupus, failure of the embryo transplant company, and frankly, I didn't feel so good about myself. We sold the small animal clinic to devote more time to an embryo transfer project. That ended up enriching my professional acumen but drained most of our financial resources.

After the sale of the practice we weren't broke, just bent out of shape. Zandy was hoping we could go back to Ohio, with a preference to the Ohio Valley. Southeast Ohio was where she wanted to spend her remaining days; however long it would be.

The plan was for me to go to this part of the country to find out if we could survive. It looked very promising, but this was Appalachia with an unemployment rate as one of the highest in the state.

It was a good plan, and if I had a chance to reconsider, I would do it over again. The people I met in Berg County convinced me this was a caring community. Friendships quickly became extraordinarily friendships. The Marcus Weisshut family is a good example of many to choose from to weave this story.

Marcus Weisshut was the client every veterinarian dreams of having. Marcus would be a success no matter what vocation he chose. He was a farmer along the Ohio River in the Berg County hills. Everything in Berg County is hilly; it is called, "The Switzerland of Ohio."

His show cows were Simmentals, a Swiss breed, outstanding in quality and they were big! Participating in perhaps ten county fairs and three state fairs was a family event every summer. The teenagers Michael and "Missy" took charge of showing the animals while Marcus and his wife Belle manned a mobile western goods store that drew old friends to their trailer.

The Weisshut stores served as the only western goods stores in Southeastern Ohio. The home store was at their farm. Prices were more than fair, so both venues were very busy. It seemed that every person that knew the Weisshuts considered them family.

Farming in Berg County was mostly raising cattle to graze the green hills moistened by significant rainfall. There was a lot of hay to make during the summer to feed the livestock the rest of the year. Big round bales of hay weighing half a ton were a part of the pastoral landscape.

Because of the hills and problems of erosion, it was necessary to practice contour farming. The long sweeping curves of pastures between the ever-present trees of the Wayne National Forest made Berg County a destination magnet for visitors in the fall for some of the best fall foliage colors in the country.

November weather in Berg County was damp, muddy, and chilly. Marcus set the schedule to pregnancy check several cows at his farm November 7th, my fifty-fourth birthday. Palpating for pregnancy in cows was a common job that helped planning for shows later in the year. Having a calf during a show disrupts everything about showing animals, including the owner, so we needed to know.

There were six cows in a holding stall to palpate. The first five moved from the holding pen where we caught them one at a time in the outdoor chute and did the pregnancy checks on them. The sixth cow decided not to go that way, so she went back to the herd.

This particular cow was the Grand Champion at the Pennsylvania, West Virginia, and the Ohio State Fairs. Missy at thirteen showed her at all three fairs, so this cow was something special, and she apparently knew it. The second time we tried to coax her through the gate, it turned into a nightmare.

My job was simply to stand at the end of a swinging gate to keep the cow from getting through. No problem: our recalcitrant critter came through anyway. Not only did our cow come through; she put her head down and lifted it as we collided. Her head came up with the poll (the top between where the horns would be, except she had no horns) and connected with my sternum and moved up to slam into my jaw.

There was no sensation of pain, only the feeling my body was taking a trip somewhere. I was flying through the air.

My back hit the side of the barn nine feet above the driveway, making a dirty boot outline of the toes pointing to each side. The boot marks were eleven feet high and twenty-two feet from where the cow hit me. That was evidence enough to validate that my body indeed made an unintended journey to a place far from where I was standing just a few seconds earlier.

As my body dropped to the ground, "17" came after me and butted all my one hundred and ninety pounds out of the barnyard and down a hill. For some strange reason, there was an awareness of what was happening.

The ear tag with the number 17 became a vision that I can still resurrect from the recesses of my brain at will. Again, there was no pain. I was somehow observing the attack in every detail from a point thirty feet above the ground. The show played in my head in slow motion. That was more than strange!

Marcus caught up with "17" with a pitchfork in his hands and started hitting the cow with it. She turned on Marcus and ran over him. I "watched" the slow-motion video in my head as the "17" broke Marcus's left femur with a compound fracture.

"17" turned her attention to me again and continued pushing my body to the bottom of the hill alongside a wood plank fence. "17" was exhausted. She had me straddled with her face pressing on my chest.

Suddenly there was pain, joining what a moment before was a silent movie. Talk about panic! Conciseness was confusing. I woke up with a cow pushing down on my chest, blowing snot in my face, and everything hurt. My confused brain didn't know at first if I was dead or alive. Was I dead and went to hell? What was the crazed cow doing here with me? The thought of eternity with a mad cow was frightening! Was her only task to be my tormentor for eternity? Eternity was a long time.

At that instant, (or was it an eternity?) scenes of my life as a boy raced through my head. I especially noted in slow motion my First Communion day, standing in the farm garden next to the gravel road, watching my uncle Vernon, my godfather, coming to visit us on my special day My godfather was supposed to be in heaven.

There was no bright shining light, but there was a message, "It is not time. You have a family that needs you." With that, I was fully alert, alive, and in excruciating pain, but able to move.

The cow was so tired that her legs were locked outward and it was my body that was holding her head up. She wasn't pushing; she was resting. I managed to wiggle out from under her head and crawl away from her. She still didn't move. It was when I reached the fence and stood up as best I could that Marcus shouted, "Look out Doc! She 's coming at you again!"

With that, a superhuman effort on my part got me over the fence and on the other side on the ground. A crash at the wooden fence followed as "17" smashed several fence boards. One of the planks about five feet long landed on my feet. I picked up the plank and was ready to go to war with the cow. Both the cow and I were still breathing hard. "17" was standing at the hole in the fence.

Marcus came hobbling down the rest of the way to where we were. "Sorry, didn't mean to make your cow mad," I said through great gasps for air. He was gasping for air too as he said, "Don't worry about her. Are you OK?" "No, I said, but you are hurt more than I am. You may have a compound fractured, broken femur." Earlier in my silent movie, I saw the bone protruding outside the skin. "We have to get you to the hospital," I think I said.

There was no broken leg as it turned out, but he was run over by "17" and suffered at least a bruise along with bright red blood soaking his coveralls.

Marcus marveled that I "saw" the cow attack him. So was I. There are times I think none of this happened, but x-rays proved it did. I had fractures of the lateral processes on each side of the third cervical vertebra (that's the neck), and before a storm hits to this day, my neck goes crazy with shots of pain radiating all the way from my neck to my feet.

As the two of us hobbled past "17", she was looking like a very sick cow. The neck chain tag really was a 17. Trying to put things in a believable perspective was too much to process. Taking care of Marcus and his injured leg called for routine care, a lot easier on my tired brain.

His family got him out of his coveralls to find there was more bleeding than expected. Belle cut his pants leg off to expose the wound and started to clean the leg and put pressure on the squirting artery. Michael went to my vehicle with me to get all the supplies to fix his dad's leg for the ride to the nearby hospital in Parkersburg, West Virginia. Belle joked that it was good to see Marcus treated like a dog.

Everything was under control. Even the two Tylenol extra strength capsules were helping enough to think about driving home.

I drove home to lie down, intending to go to the nearest county hospital directly but fatigue dictated differently. I woke up in my dirty work clothes the next morning with Denna the receptionist making noises in the clinic on the first floor.

"How did I drive back to town?" I thought. My last memory was stopping for a deer in the road a mile north of the farm.

She demanded every last detail about what happened and that I needed to get to a doctor to find out what works and how badly I was injured. She told me I looked like an old bull rider.

The drive to the hospital was twenty-five miles of twisted highway. It felt like a two hundred mile trip. Admission to the emergency hospital seemed routine with a nurse taking my temperature and my clothes. Another nurse said they were busy but just rest and that they would take care of me as quickly as they could.

Three hours passed, and I read all the Sports Illustrated and hunting magazines in the hospital. Nobody talked to me anymore, so I found my clothes, put them on and opened the window and left. I left the window open just to let the hospital staff know there was a person in there for some reason.

On the way out of town, the game warden was checking a line of deer hunters registering their deer killed. It then dawned on me that this was the first day of deer hunting. Hunting season in Southeastern Ohio was very much like a celebration of a national holiday. Everything stops, so I suspect every doctor at the hospital was out deer hunting. Hospital services in this part of the state sucks. I should know; I was the county health commissioner in a neighboring county that didn't even have a hospital. My experience reminded me again that this was Appalachia, not unlike a third world country.

The next day was spent being a health commissioner. There would not be a vet call unless something bigger than deer season came up. The light duty was a relief, but boring. I even entertained the idea of buying a hunting license.

Meanwhile, three weeks later, cow Number "17" was still wandering the woods on the Weisshut farm since the episode before she came home on her own. Marcus had enough with her mean streak. She was not the gentle show cow that Missy took care of at the fair.

Pregnant or not, she was headed to the auction. Belle's brother was a cattle truck driver, so when he came to load "17" into the truck, she balked. The chute up into the cattle truck was steep and narrow, but somehow, "17" turned around in the tight space and headed out the chute.

Marcus had a big Massey Harris tractor with a cab that he used to block "17" from turning around and escaping again. That didn't work so well either. Once "17" got to the truck bed, she turned around again to face the tractor. Without hesitation, she jumped on top of the tractor and through the cab and right over Marcus. This time she messed up a leg, and it wasn't hers. Her legs took her back out to the woods.

Marcus now had another hit to his left leg, but I didn't see it happen this time.

Michael kept an eye on "17" for the rest of the winter as she roamed the hills like a wild animal, She would soon have her calf, so she needed to come to the barn for protection from the weather. That happened without any drama on her part, and she had a nice heifer calf.

When these Simmental cows have their babies, we expect that the hormonal changes at birthing make them aggressive for about three days, and then everything gets back to normal.

"17" wasn't normal. She was aggressive and continued being aggressive. She lost weight and roamed aimlessly, displaying the behavior associated with a disease called Listeriosis.

The disease affects the blood vessels in the brain and is responsible for a high percentage of abortions, so there was some doubt that this might not be Listeriosis since she didn't abort her calf.

There was no way to get close enough to give an injection of antibiotic unless we used a dart gun, and by now, I doubt we could help her. Her baby was nursing another cow so the calf would be OK.

"17" had plenty of energy to escape again. Michael had enough. This cow injured every member of the family. He was going to find her and put her out of her misery. When he did find her, she was already dead.

We had a mini-seminar at the house about everything known about Listeriosis and decided upon changes in the storage practice of the big round bales of hay. We knew that rotted vegetation fostered growth of the Listeriosis bacteria. The result of the mini-seminar was deciding the problem as wet, rotten hay in the bales left unprotected during winter. The solution was to keep the feed dry. The farmers figured out how to get that done.

The neighboring farmers reported that a lot of deer died in a similar manner as Marcus' cow. It was common to see herds of deer on the Weisshut farm that numbered over fifty animals in a group. They ate a lot of the hay bales lying in the fields. We called the game warden in on the issue.

Testing for this disease on a cow dead for several days was not likely to come up with a positive result. We collected blood, manure, and spinal fluid. The state agricultural diagnostic lab results were negative.

A new technique called polymerase chain reaction offered by a federal lab ran the test on the spinal fluid and reported a definite positive for Listeriosis.

Listeriosis affected people, so our Health Department got involved by writing a series of news releases concerning how humans and animals became infected. We described how the disease worked in the victims, how to prevent it and how it spreads. It was interesting that ninety percent of the questions the health department fielded came from hunters.

The reports of deer dying from suspected Listeriosis fell off to zero. The factors killing deer in Berg County now are cars and poachers, and then hunters. Listeriosis was estimated to rank as number three in that order before we understood the nature of a disease caused by tiny bacteria.

Weekend at the (Ohio) River

What does a health commissioner do on his weekends? The early summer of 1988 was spent doing a lot of official stuff to keep the population healthy around the southeastern part of the county. One of the nastiest tasks was removing dead cows from the near vicinity of people's homes. Complaints were a daily event, including weekends. You might wonder why the farmers didn't take on that responsibility. Let me explain.

For the last eight years, the Greyhound racing community at Wheeling Island Downs and the Berg County farmers had a strange relationship, maybe even macabre. Racing and training Greyhound dogs required a diet of up to sixty percent ground hamburger while they were working. Two pounds a day at the cost of ground beef was so expensive that the track would shut down within a week. Fortunately, the nearby Berg County farmers had thousands of live cows and lots of dead ones as well.

A neighborhood slaughterhouse contracted to supply racing dog ground beef from downer cows and those that died from lightning. Meat from a diseased animal never was processed for any use as food for people and animals according to the state statutes. There was no spoiled beef involved; just cheap racing Greyhound hamburger mixed with charcoal so people wouldn't eat it.

The slaughterhouse produced no other business other than the dog food. One of our missions at the health department was to send our inspector to the facility monthly to fulfill the State Health Department mandate for meat inspection. We had to make certain none of this meat was reaching the human population.

The butcher made his daily rounds to pick up and haul away the carcass to his slaughterhouse for processing. The farmer had a free service in the quick disposal of the dead cow, and the butcher had a decent business with the Greyhound trainers.

This business was symbiosis in a business sense, and it was too good to last. A small group of local PETA (People for the Ethical Treatment of Animals) thought this collaboration was abhorrent, so they harassed both the racetrack and the slaughterhouse. The group directed their effort to the slaughterhouse.

Within a week, the equipment from the old facility moved across the Ohio River to West Virginia where there were just as many dead cows to prepare over there. The dead cow butcher then continued to sell West Virginia beef to the Greyhound people.

The cattle owners had to revert to their previous creative thinking after losing the service of their dead cow disposal. Some of the Berg County farmers dug holes to bury their dead stock, but that was too costly, and soon the general practice was to drag the carcass to the woods to let them rot.

Some of the dead cows found their way to the doorsteps of the five PETA organizers repeatedly who then backed off with a public statement that they were wrong with their action, an epic first recanting for PETA!

The dead cows at the doorsteps ceased, but the woods continued to smell of dead cows. Now it was the Berg County Health Commissioner's job to clean up the mess.

We thought we had the solution to the problem by offering a free landfill burial site for dead cows. The owner of any dead cows brought the carcass to a trailer or truck bed and dumped their load to the county landfill dedicated offloading site for free.

A monster storm system dumped on us with a week of downpour storms and thousands of lightning strikes. I can attest to a significant increase for vet calls to verify lightning strikes for the insurance companies. It became difficult to remove the carcasses from the pastures and woods.

Something bad had to happen with all the mud and misery. One cow got away on us! This cow was a lightning casualty and rolled down into a creek bed. I did the report on this animal for the farmer as a confirmed lightning strike for the insurance to pay just the day before. The stream was rushing halfway to the top when I examined the dead cow.

Later, the rain filled the creek and apparently washed the cow towards the Ohio River. All day Friday, the Health Department received calls as to the movement of the cow for the three miles before it got into the Ohio River.

Somehow a dead cow floating in a major waterway during a flood became the sheriff's responsibility along with that of the health department, quickly followed by the TV stations.

We had it covered, well, maybe not. The plan was to locate the floating carcass, pull it to shore and secure it to the shore out of the mainstream of the river. A boat was available to tow the cow to the landing of one of my vet customers, Mike who operated a river barge tow business.

Mike had all the equipment to lift the dead cow out of the river with his crane, onto a waiting truck and then have it hauled it to the landfill. The TV station was treating this episode as first class disaster news.

Sheriff Tink Sulsberger and I were on a boat when we located the cow already tangled in the riverside brush. Tink sat quietly looking at the situation. "It will be a bitch towing her out of that jungle, he said, unless she blows up during the night."

The next morning Mike and I took the two-mile boat ride to where we last saw the cow. There was no cow there! What greeted us was a clearing in the bushes with parts of the cow hanging in the branches for a hundred feet in all directions from where we left the cow the day before. Big catfish were skimming the surface, fighting over the fragments of flesh not only of the cow but also of dozens of dead catfish from the explosion. Dead cows don't blow up like that unless a charge of dynamite is involved.

I told Mike that I wanted to look around for a minute. I mentioned my conversation with Tink the day before and had thoughts that maybe Tink beat us to the cow.

"You know, Mike said, if it were up to me, I would get out my bow and fit an arrow with a charge and blow that cow up myself." He added, " I grew up with that guy, and you're right. Let's get rid of the evidence for him."

Sure enough, there was part of an arrow shaft with the fletching attached, floating in the middle of the newly cleared cove.

Mike went to church and then delivered the present to Tink. My job was to meet the TV crew to tell them everything was OK and the cow was gone. Questions flew, and I told them that it wasn't a pretty sight; nothing I would want to see on my TV on Sunday morning.

KaBoom, Swoosh

The fascinating part of being the health commissioner was fielding complaints by Berg County residents. By law, the Health Department had to reply to any complaint within ten days by personally contacting the person serving the complaint, investigate the situation, and finally, resolve the condition or send it up to a higher jurisdiction, usually the State of Ohio Department of Health.

We settled almost all complaints within the ten days. Maybe that was because there wasn't anything else to do, but I think it was due to the cooperation of all the other resources in the community being willing to pitch in and help, especially the Sheriff's Office.

This complaint of the day dealt with a licensed but primitive recycling station in the southern part of the county. A nearby homeowner complained that the stacked up paper and cardboard was drawing unwelcome residents, namely rats and snakes. In her complaint, the lady reported the operator was abusive and obstinate.

Charlie, our health department field investigator (along with several other titles) was sent to get some information, and we would talk more about what we could do.

When Charlie returned, he said that there was a little war brewing down there. The woman filing the complaint was angry but afraid of the recycling site operator because he just got released from the state prison. He murdered a man and stuffed his body down an abandoned oil well casing was the story Charlie brought back to the office.

I contacted Sheriff Sulsberger, (or "Tink," as we called him) and asked if he could give us some information on how to proceed with our complaint. The Sheriff said he was free to take me down to the recycling yard and fill me in during the drive.

It seemed that our two-time "Best Sheriff in the USA" recipient recently took more interest in the operations of the health department than it deserved, so I asked him about it when he arrived ten minutes later. "No, he said, you people just have the propensity to get your nose into more interesting stuff. It gets boring for a small- town sheriff around here."

The car the sheriff drove was an older model Cadillac that he claimed could go 160 miles an hour, and not only was it an unmarked car, but the tags and VIN also did not exist. "You certainly didn't go that fast on the highways of Berg County," I said. "No, the sheriff replied, it was at Cadiz and the roads there aren't as nice as we have here. I did hit 120 miles per hour on the Half-Mile Straightaway chasing after a new red Mustang if you're interested. I caught the sucker too."

My friends tell me that Sheriff Sulsberger, "Tink" doesn't brag. "He's a legend around here," my friend Perry said. Legend or not, Tink did his share of bragging.

The recycling yard was a disaster. The woman had reason to complain. Rats were visible in the middle of the day, running through the piles of loose cardboard.

Tink said, "Let me talk to him, Keep quiet until I introduce you to him. He's a sensitive man." Joe Wartz was respectful to the sheriff, and the two talked about at least six people that all seemed to be on parole. The State released Joe on parole after serving thirty years in the state penitentiary for murder.

Joe had enough money from a state grant to start up a small business recycling waste materials, but he knew nothing of running a business. It appeared he was doing extremely well, collecting waste paper, cans, and glass.

He admitted he didn't know a thing about selling the stuff. That's when Tink introduced me to Joe, saying, "Doc Tebbe is the health commissioner, maybe he can help you with that part." Boy, he set me up!

Pretty soon it was clear that the health department could help Joe.

Charlie brought several letters from two recycling companies to my attention within the last month, one from Youngstown and another from Pittsburgh.

Both wanted to connect to small collectors to take their material, so I told him about that, and added, "I am sure they want the paper stuff baled. Joe crushed the glass bottles and put it in wood crates that the companies provide, same with the cans.

"Yeah, he happily added, that's what we are doing with the glass," I explained that baling the paper is not a problem. It takes metal straps that tighten the paper products with a hand jack. I offered to help him set up the paper baling, but it required that Joe had to build a pen to contain the paper.

"You also should try to be kind to your neighbor who has been complaining to us that she is scared of you," I added since it was his neighbor that started this investigation, and she needed to be satisfied.

"Aw, I don't know how to speak to people, you know. I ain't seen a woman in thirty years, and she scares me to death," He said.

I told him that Charlie works with me and he will be the person helping him. I promised Joe I would keep in touch to see how he progressed and added, "Charlie is a good man so take good care of him, OK?"

Tink hadn't said a word during my conversation with Joe, but now he picked up on his questions again about how all the ex-cons in the county were doing. He got so much information he asked me to get a notebook from his glove box so he could write it all down.

Upon returning, the two men were talking to a hired hand (another ex-con) that was welding a chain to the corner of a shed.

I walked over to the rat infested pile of cardboard to see if it was a simple piece of work. The baled paper should take away the home of the rodents. A front-end loader on a tractor was needed to fill the box for baling. Joe had the loader and the tractor, but they were not connected.

The tractor was probably forty years old. The back wheels had iron lugs instead of rubber tires. The front wheels were also steel, perfect for crushing glass. Joe had that one figured out.

Tink was walking around the yard, and the helper went off to smoke a cigarette. Joe climbed into the tractor seat and started to crush a pile of beer and whiskey bottles with the steel wheels. When he finished, there was enough glass to fill a pickup truck bed. It was incredible how Joe was able to get so much work done with junk equipment.

A shout interrupted the quiet (call it a cuss word) followed by a loud Boom! The tractor got too close to the acetylene tank that the helper left next to the pile of glass. Evidently, the front wheels hit the tank a glancing blow. In rapid succession, one of the back wheels ran over the top part of the tank, knocking it off the main part of the gas container. Woosh!!! The tank started to spin.

Joe jumped off the tractor and ran for his life. The tractor was still moving. Then the tank hit the tractor wheel again, setting it to a launch position, and launch it did!

Like a rocket propelled by the escaping gas, it headed for the neighbor's house. The missile clipped the corner of the dwelling on the second floor, taking out most of a bedroom and then continued south toward the Ohio River in a high arc.

The river was almost a quarter mile from the house, and the Ohio River at this place was a good half-mile wide. The white steam trail of the rocket started to drop and made it to the West Virginia half of the Ohio River.

Joe didn't stop running until the tank descended into the river. He probably thought the tank was going to hunt him down or something. The helper was gone too. You could see the dust of his old pickup truck tearing off up the road. Tink and I both stood transfixed like kids watching Fourth of July fireworks.

The tractor was slowly heading for trouble, so I caught up to it and turned off the ignition switch. The recycling yard had the same Allis Chalmers tractor I grew up with on our family farm thirty-five years ago. Our tractor was ancient then.

After the excitement, the neighbor came out of her house shaking. Tink spoke with her for a moment. He was saying, "You should expect the insurance company to repair the damage and get a brand new bedroom out of this. Call your insurance man and tell him that Tink says he can call it an "Act of God.""

The lady was so star-struck that the famous Sheriff of Berg County had spoken to her. She was not concerned about her house or her danger. She expressed concern for that poor junk mans' safety.

The Health Department staff fulfilled the promises to Joe. There was enough junk lumber on his property to build a pretty neat box to secure the paper products for Joe to tighten the straps. His bales were close enough to the size specified by the company from Youngstown.

The only snake, anybody, saw was a big fat gopher snake, a harmless species that lives off rats in the absence of gophers. The rat problem stopped, and the recycling yard passed Charlie's inspections. Joe didn't make much money, but he kept busy and happy for the help from the sheriff and the "Health Guys."

The neighbor lady did get a new bedroom out of the accident and was happy also for the extermination of the rats. She hated rats, and Joe wasn't such a bad guy after all. She withdrew her complaint when Joe finally finished cleaning up his yard.

HEALTH COMMISSIONER APPOINTMENT

Berg County had a health problem when I first came to Walden. It had more to do with the scarcity of medical doctors than with unhealthy people. A young doctor after a couple of years as a private practitioner and part time public health commissioner recently vacated the town. A new Health Commissioner had to be appointed to replace the doctor who left town. The only other medical doctor in the county had a busy private practice and he had no interest in making any changes by adding public health challenges.

The county's sole veterinarian qualified for the requirements of being a health commissioner, but he was retired and had no interest. A nurse with a master's degree in public health would be eligible, but there were none available.

There was only one medical professional with qualifications to serve as the health commissioner; not by my talents, but more so as being a warm body living in the county; a requirement by law. The Board of Health didn't even ask for my resume.

The board members felt that having a veterinarian as the health commissioner was a step backward professionally. I did my homework and was able to relate some facts about the veterinary curriculum and the strong emphasis on public health. Ten percent of my class was currently health commissioners in Ohio. If we counted my classmates in the military as medical directors and other public health services, almost one quarter of my class were involved in public health.

To protect the population from health problems, especially in the human food supply and zoonotic diseases (contacted from animals) was the first two mandates listed in the expectations of a veterinarian upon graduation. After all, more than two hundred diseases made the list of zoonotic diseases, and most were pretty serious.

The position was interesting but it only paid $630.00 a month as a part-time health commissioner. The part time medical doctor who preceded me was paid five times that much and left town for better opportunities.

The president of the Berg County Board of Health suggested the possibility of supplementing the offered salary by writing grants that would bring more federal and state money to the budget of the health department. He said that ten percent of the grants included management costs that would bring my income up dramatically.

I would like to share my first recollection of my experiences as a health commissioner about that man, the President of the Board of health, Damian Shultz.

Mr. Shultz was a Christian Fundamentalist preacher/politician first and an elementary school teacher secondly. A small man in stature with a scholarly presence; it was a surprise to find him so overbearing and ambitious. I immediately disliked the man and did not trust him.

Through the years and by the time we met he had a long list of political favors of many township trustees and appointees that he called upon to support his issues.

Mr. Schultz was a Republican. I believe he was the only Republican in the county. I would have joined him since at the time I was also a registered Republican, and that had to change. To get the position I had to agree to change my affiliation to become a Democrat. That was important. That was also strange, but as I spent more time in Berg County, I began to understand how political the place was!

His ambition was to become the county's health commissioner for some reason. He declared that wish publicly. That too was strange because he did not possess a single attribute to qualify for the position except residency.

For the first time in my life that I am aware of, someone, this man, considered me an enemy. I didn't take the job to spite Mr. Schultz. I accepted it because it was an opportunity to help the community and I felt comfortable with its challenges.

The staff in the health department helped complete several grants within my first year as health commissioner. The amount that would come to the board of health for administration of the two grants would be enough to make a difference for the underpaid staff.

That was what I hoped would happen. The board saw it differently and reluctantly approved receiving the grant dealing with smokeless tobacco in the schools. The second program was thought too sensitive and was rejected by the board after they read the prospectus.

Mr. Shultz was quite agitated that our data on the smokeless tobacco use in the schools showed that the school he taught in, and specifically his third grade classroom, had the highest percentage of children users. Former students were presenting with oral cancer lesions and one died before he finished the seventh grade.

Mr. Schultz felt he was singled out as being responsible for the problem in Berg County. His school wasn't the only one using smokeless tobacco in the county. Five teachers in his school, and just as many in the other county schools including Damian Schultz, indicated they were smokeless tobacco users, but not in the classroom.

It turned out that using "snuse" in the classroom was all too common. The data were incriminating so the health education program was implemented. There was truly a serious health issue in all of Appalachia concerning using smokeless tobacco that needed to be at least confronted.

Our program was funded annually with six more Appalachian counties in Ohio following suit with our program template, bringing evidence of the dangers of smokeless tobacco in students in all grades. It was no longer "cool" for a kid to have that ring of weathered hip pocket cloth from his or her can of "snuse".

The second grant unsuccessfully implemented was a program fashioned after one the school system in Phoenix introduced a decade earlier and was still running continuously with the help of the police departments. The program was called, "Mr. Stranger Danger". It addressed the pedophile problem at schools. It was not intentionally first implemented at Mr. Shultz's elementary school. In fact, there was no indication of child abuse in the county officially.

We first researched the value of this program at the request of a small group of parents who guaranteed that the facts would never surface without such a program placed in the schools and overseen by local police officers and sheriff deputies

The parents were right. Once the law enforcement people were involved it was clearly recognized as a problem that had been covered up. Unfortunately, once the allegations of sex abuse were raised, an angry cloud persisted in an otherwise quiet community.

That was what Mr. Schultz was worried about. The local weekly newspaper found this information sensational and pounded the board as to why they didn't support the grant. The heat from the newspaper was probably excessive, and finally, the Sheriff's office announced they would investigate all their data on pedophiles living in the county and have that information available to the public.

That satisfied the worried parents, the Health Department, the newspaper, and the sheriff's office, but not everybody. There wasn't a big exodus, but enough to convince me not to apply for a grant like that again.

At the next board meeting I asked for a raise for all the staff. That didn't go over very well.

By this time the politics of poor counties were completely revealed to me as a dependent population receiving huge amounts of money per capita by way of grants, title funds and welfare. The programs were certainly needed and local input was part of administering this money. Many programs were well managed to provide help for education, job training and health services.

Not all departments were managed like that. Some were managed to get more and more funding every year, even if last year's budget had a surplus. A percentage; usually ten percent of any federal and state funding went to administration specifically.

As more funding found its way into local programs, that ten percent too often ended up in the favorite frills of the people in charge. This created little political fiefdoms for the local boards in too many community services. The board of health was a good example of that practice.

I was tired of small town politicians milking the system like gangsters. My plan was to resign if there would be no support from the other board members. They were all aware Mr. Schultz was part of the problem. If they supported him and accepted my resignation, I certainly did not want to serve as health commissioner in a community that allowed that kind of administration. They supported Mr. Schultz and accepted my resignation three to two in a vote.

My next step was to visit my counselor, the sheriff. He told me, "It's a lot like I told your boy, leave town and behave yourself." He thought my life and that of Zandy were in danger.

"People with less provocation than you've handed to the board have ended up dead in this county. Tink said, You don't have to fight them. Sooner or later their power blows away and I think the parents of those kids will get their revenge. You certainly got the people's attention." He promised his staff would do what had to be done, but expected it would cost him his election, so he planned to retire, himself. This was from a twice-selected "Best Sheriff in America".

That experience sent a whole bunch of plans to a sudden stop. At fifty-four years old, there were responsibilities to my family. My first name may be Don, but Quixote is not my last name. Zandy had leased our house in Arizona at the end of the school year and joined me. She was busy with substitute teaching in the middle grades in Berg County when the school session started in the fall.

One of the schools she substituted for was Mr. Schultz's school. Evidentially she had a confrontation precipitated by Mr. Schultz that ended with Zandy calling him "an evil, evil man". Her expectations of staying in Walden took a sudden turn, and the message from the cow attack was still fresh in my mind, "It is not time to pass. Your family needs you", made our decision. Plans were made to move back to Arizona.

How did it turn out? I'm not sure, but the community is still standing. Some of the best people in America still live there. The health commissioner is a woman who is doing a great job, especially for the poor citizens. Hopefully she has no enemies. And by the way, the smokeless tobacco program is still in place.

Mr. Schultz never became the health commissioner. The last I heard, he was a sick man.

The county is still a beautiful place to live. Maybe I did precipitate some good things for the people living there. They certainly deserved more than the gift of living in a beautiful place. The population dropped twenty percent with the recession of 2008, but is coming back.

Something important changed the county around the turn of the century, hopefully for the better. When the technology called "fracking" finally reached Berg County, the farms had a new cash crop: natural gas. The county added two thousand new millionaires and growing.

I never had the vision to change the place, just to enjoy it. Berg County was enjoyable, but not enough to die for. My bucket list was getting shorter. There was one item in the bucket that kept popping up. Someone should write a novel set in Berg County. I don't think anybody has written a book based in Berg County. The area certainly has enough strong personalities to make it interesting.

MOLLY'S GIFT

Molly was waiting for me in the examination room, lying quietly by her owner's feet. She pulled herself up off the floor to greet me with a friendly wag and warm, lovely eyes. I recognized her owner but only in a passing manner. Margie operated a flower shop about five stores down in the same shopping center, and my attraction at her shop was the delicious homemade fudge named, "Molly McFudge" after the beautiful Golden Retriever now licking my offered hand.

The scheduled examination obviously wasn't a friendly "get to know your doctor" visit. Margie had tears sliding down her cheeks. A glance at Molly revealed swollen lymph glands at every location. I knelt to examine her further to find swelling in the front legs caused by the enlarged glands pressing against the return blood flow on its journey back to the heart.

Molly had cancer tentatively called malignant lymphosarcoma, later confirmed by tests and a radiologist specialist. Her breed was cursed with a high potential of having this type of cancer.

Since a loss of appetite and occasional throwing up were involved, it was an indication that the lymph nodes inside the body were affected as much as the obviously swollen glands on the outside.

We talked about Molly's chances for getting better. Margie knew what stage four meant regarding tumors. With a goal of reducing the size of the tumors, we could help Molly's discomfort, but it would only be temporary. Margie agreed to start with an injection of a steroid and to bring Molly to the clinic when needed.

For me, the use of steroids treating lymphatic cancer was the last resort.

Molly became comfortable for a few months with the injections or the tablet form, but the deadly side effects outweighed the benefits all too soon.

The first injection helped within 24 hours and the lumps almost disappeared. Three weeks later we checked Molly and gave another calculated dose. For three days after that treatment, Molly drank a lot of water and then settled down to normal again.

I was keenly aware of the use of steroids. For the last four months, my wife, Zandy was hospitalized for her advancing lupus. We were past the point where the treatment was far worse than the disease. Her only positive response to anything was flowers. A little bouquet every couple days brought a beaming child-like smile of awe when a nice man she didn't recognize delivered the flowers.

Margie and I had struck a deal trading vet service for flowers. As time went on, Margie brought Mollie to the vet clinic more often, and I was receiving flower arrangements from Margie's flower shop. Margie called my receptionist to let us know she would be bringing Molly over and I met her outside the clinic. Mollie was tired of getting injections and associated the vet clinic with getting those injections.

We both knew there was an end for this financial arraignment coming soon for both of us.

Both Molly and Zandy passed away within weeks. We were within eight cents between our two statements. The thought occurred that this was a good omen at a difficult time. It felt like a privilege to get to know Molly's owner over the last several months.

I was overwhelmed with funeral services, church services, extended care facility services, medical bills, overdue rent, and IRS letters. Margie took care of the flowers at the church and the funeral home. They were beyond beautiful! For a long time, I had no idea how or if I did pay for the funeral flowers.

It turned out; that beautiful florist indeed paid for the flowers and a lot more.

Even though it was tragic that my wife suffered for years, there was no real grief for the loss. Yes, there was the loss, but no real closure. A monsignor of the church who was a client and a friend sought me out to check how I was coping. We discussed the absence of grief issue. My problem was the guilt for feeling death was a relief for Zandy and me both.

Father Robert told me that for the last year grief was a daily companion, watching Zandy die a little bit every day. It made sense to me what he said, so it was time to remember the good memories, and there were many.

One day Margie asked if I would like to go for a beer at a pub down the street the next day after work. Suddenly the day became brighter. There was no way I could say, "No, thank you!"

Margie picked me up at the clinic in her daughter's Jeep. I met Jenni earlier at the flower shop and thought they were sisters. At the bar the conversation was swapping flower stories and vet stories. That was the first time in months that I laughed and enjoined being with a friend.

For a month or more after the funeral, there was a steady supply of cakes, casseroles, cards and more cards from my clients, mostly widows. One woman even proposed to me, showing her bank statement with over a million dollars balance. With that much money, it shouldn't take long before she got what she wanted, but not here! Margie was on my mind a lot.

I wanted to express my feelings, so I did. That was the best thing I've ever done. Three months later we were married. The cakes and casseroles stopped magically. Margie and I have been married for twenty-three wonderful years. When the subject comes up, she says that I am almost paid up.

BUDDY

I like to let my brain take a break and wander off sometimes. The price for daydreaming usually isn't worth the momentary pleasure. Buddy was an exception. I think of Buddy often, and find myself laughing. He was worth the diversion. In my Sun City West practice, I had a standard schnauzer on the table with the owner in front of the dog, talking to her "Buddy."

I was pulling an exam glove on when she asked, "What are you going to do with that glove?" I answered without thinking (a fault of mine) saying, "I am going to check his anal sacs."

I noticed the double-arm grip she had on Buddy and glanced at her face, which was in open-mouthed astonishment, so I asked, "Are you OK? What's wrong?" She stammered, "My Buddy doesn't do that!" By now I was confused, "He doesn't do what?" I asked. "My Buddy does not do anal sex" she spit out as she took Buddy off the table. I couldn't back pedal fast enough, but I did say something about it being an oil gland, a "sac" not sex.

The message finally was understood, but the owner was so distraught that we could not complete the exam and vaccination that day. She said, "I will be back with Buddy after I get myself together. I am so embarrassed about this I'll probably have to talk to my therapist".

Since then my choice of words changed to a more sensitive, even cultivated approach to introducing this procedure. This story was entered in a veterinary publication asking for the most embarrassing event as a veterinarian. They received thirty-seven same stories. We were all given first place.

Ostrich Ranching in Arizona

Jesse Sannoval was in the reception room, entertaining my staff with stories about ostriches. When I came out of the exam room, Jesse introduced himself with a strong handshake for such a little guy. In his other hand was a piece of metal panel from a golf cart, sporting a jagged rip about ten inches long from top to bottom. "I brought this along to see if you would be interested to have our ostrich operation as a client," he said.

Jesse explained that the golf cart panel was a serious reminder of the dangers that that go along with working with ostriches. The damaged panel of the rear of the golf cart caught the wrath of one of the male ostriches after Jesse snatched an egg in a pen holding a breeding pair of ostriches.

The male ran up to the golf cart and with a forward strike, ripped the metal panel with his middle toenail. That toenail had the density of flint. The sheet of metal was the same as Honda automobiles had as their side panels. The metal panel was pretty messed up.

The fertile eggs, like the one Jesse stole from the male ostrich, were incubated in their hatchery. Any new eggs from that pair will naturally stay with the ostrich pair because of the danger that male showed. The ostrich pair took turns setting on the eggs until the eggs hatch.

The fertile eggs were the valuable assets producing income. The hatchery incubation success was thirty percent better than natural incubation, so it was important to nurture every egg through the steps to become a healthy ostrich in the growing flock. It was not worth getting killed, however!

Jesse and his parents started an ostrich breeding business and one of the first items to secure was a veterinarian, especially since everything was new to them too. Jesse's search for a veterinarian took less time than he expected. As it turned out, I was probably the only veterinarian in the state who was interested in ostrich care, and our clinic had the closest veterinarian, only five miles away from their ostrich ranch.

This shouldn't be as dangerous as being in charge of working with rough stock for rodeo animals, which I considered, but thought better. Those bulls were big boogers and my neck reminds me of that cow in Ohio that worked me over ten years earlier. For some reason, the chance to work with ostriches was fascinating. We shook hands on a trial for both parties.

The Sannoval's ostrich enterprise was a godsend for my newly established veterinary clinic in Sun City West, Arizona and they benefited from the 24-hour veterinary emergency service.

Their investment was substantial and incredibly demanding, both physically and mentally. Within six months they had twenty breeding pens built and another twenty pens that held growing chicks and juvenile birds.

Young ostriches became sexually mature when they were three years old for females and a year longer for the males. They lived a long productive life when healthy; as long as 35 years. Forty eggs per hen in a year were a reasonable expectation, and a profitable one. Unfortunately, there was no way to predict if a hen laid zero eggs or eighty.

The Sannoval Ranch enjoyed a very good survival rate on the chicks. Soon there were several hundred birds on the ranch, mostly young birds under a year old.

Breeding females (hens) sold for as much as forty thousand dollars in 1994, but usually closer to ten thousand dollars, which was still a lot. Males sold for about ten thousand or less and were sold as a group of several females and one male so such a sales package cost an investor at least thirty thousand dollars. By the time the young birds were mature and ready to sell in three to four years, they were selling for half that amount. We were experiencing a "fad" enterprise and investors were advised that these prices for breeding stock would not continue.

The shining star for the fledgling industry was that the large number of offspring were a source of high quality meat and exceptionally high quality leather hides, lending credibility that there was value beyond just selling breeding birds.

My learning curve came early and lasted for years. Veterinary skills for ostriches were much like those for large and small animals, but handling a four hundred pound ostrich as tall as six or seven feet and a lot faster than any farm animal was a challenge. They hit forty miles per hour within a few seconds and maintained that speed for more than an hour!

The secret to handle ostriches was to go slow and crowd the ostrich patient into a corner and hug with downward pressure over the wings. As much as possible, I tried to have someone else do that, so I was able to use both hands to do my job.

Taking blood samples and implanting microchips were simple and quick procedures. Suturing lacerations was always done with someone holding the ostrich quietly for what could be a long time, while I gave local anesthesia, cleaned the wound and sutured away. I never had an ostrich get away during a surgery. Once the ostrich was comfortable being held, there was no struggle.

If an ostrich ran crazy at over 40 mph and crashed into a fence, the ostrich always had massive damage compared to the fence.

A common problem requiring surgery was to remove foreign objects from the "crop". This was the first stop for everything birds send down their esophagus. In an ostrich, that journey was about three feet long.

With ostriches' obsession with anything shiny, or other strange stuff, the lightning-fast reaction was to swallow it. Sometimes the object got caught in the mid esophagus, and the only option for relief was surgery.

Mostly, foreign objects made it to the crop. If the object clogged the crop, the ostrich stopped eating. Again, the only option was surgical excision to make an opening and remove things like somebody's t-shirt, weeds that tangle into a ball, and the all-time most common item, shiny glasses, especially sun glasses. Fortunately, ostriches healed well and quickly from surgery.

On a different ostrich ranch near Wickenburg I learned another trick to subdue an anxious ostrich. I was called to do some routine blood sampling and microchip placing for a new group of thirty young adult birds. Ten were males and twenty were females that were just purchased and placed in a paddock of about three acres in size. Ordinarily, that was too much open space to safely work with big ostriches.

I was hesitant to work with those birds because they were placed together to let them socialize for the first time while their testosterone and estrogen respectively got sorted out. In time they chose their mate. Ostriches mate for life.

The juvenile male ostriches were very much like young men with the same problem with their hormones. The ostriches were strong, fully grown, aggressive, unpredictable, and they weighed four hundred pounds, so they were pretty formidable.

I noted the redness on the legs of the males that I took as a signal to leave them alone. The redder the legs became, the more aggressive the ostrich was.

The ranch hands were Mexicans and they assured me it would be safe for the "avestruz" and for us. I do not own a very big Spanish vocabulary, but I picked up the conversation where they were referring to my being a "little sister", so I told them in English, which they were fluent in, saying, "OK. Show me how you would handle the birds."

Show me they did. There were six of us, including me. One was my recorder of the information on every individual ostrich in the paddock. I collected a blood sample for medical reasons but also to have a genetic record. We verified their microchip identification with a microwave reader and examined the birds for any abnormalities.

Three men held the birds and another man called "Sirocco" who had a unique skill. His job was to sneak up to an ostrich from the side, distract it with a sparkling trinket on a string attached to a foot-long stick with one hand and when the ostrich's head came down close enough, Sirocco whopped it on the top of the bird's head with a lightweight hollow cardboard tube.

Immediately the head came up, the ostrich made a circle, landing with a soft thud on the ground, and he or she was out cold. We had three minutes of subdued bird to do everything we needed in that time. Usually we were working on the next bird by the time the last one was recovering.

A video of an ostrich as it came out of this form of sedation would be great material for America's Funniest Home Videos. First the head popped straight up again, looked around, and the ostrich promptly stood up, ruffled its feathers and ran to the rest of the flock as if nothing happened. We were done in two hours for a job I figured would take most of a day!

I'm not sure of my grip on Mexican Spanish, but the workers also called Sirocco, "The Assassin"

I was curious why the ostrich responded to a light tap on the top of the head like that. Finally, a friend who worked at the Wildlife World Zoo on the west side of Phoenix explained it for me. He said. "The brain of an ostrich is not only small. It's almost flat, about the size of a fat nickel. I don't know if it has all the essential parts, but it works for ostriches, which is the closest living thing to the dinosaur ".

Evidently, the rap on the head disrupted the nerve impulses through the "brain" enough to interfere with musculoskeletal control. In time, the neural messages reconstructed their normal pathways and the body functions recovered.

Watching an ostrich, I often wondered if they were capable of thinking, but they had plenty of pure reaction. To me it looked like there was no time at all between stimulus and reaction to think things through.

Two years after meeting Jesse, the ostrich presence in my veterinary practice had grown to clients in every county and several states. I believe it had little to do with my expertise with the big birds and a lot about other veterinarians' aversion to these dangerous beasts.

Arizona emu and ostrich growers formed a co-op, numbering 200 growers. The prices for breeding pairs were holding up but not the frantic heyday of ridiculously high prices. The membership understood that the future of ostrich farming was in the sale of meat, hides, and surprisingly, feathers.

The University of Arizona Poultry Science Department guided us through the necessary steps to be certified USDA meat inspected so the meat could be shipped interstate for restaurants all over the country.

The need for raising funds followed the organization of the co-op. One of the growers, a retired fireman, offered the use of his food truck as a kitchen on wheels. We decided to serve ostrich tenderloin sandwiches at the Chandler Arizona Ostrich Festival.

To describe those sandwiches made my mouth water. We started with the biggest Texas size buns, lightly toasted and topped with a patty of ostrich meat pounded thin, and coated with milk and egg. This was followed by panko breading and dipped in the deep fryer that we kept fresh by changing the oil three times a day. A large piece of lettuce, a big slice of giant sweet onion, and a fresh-cut tomato slice topped it off. We served the creation with or without mayonnaise to finish the package.

My guess is at least twelve hundred Calories went through the sales window once a minute on one of the fundraising ventures at the annual rock and gem show in Quartzsite. After that show there was no need for any more fundraisers.

In 1994 and 1995 I served as president of the Arizona Emu and Ostrich Co-op. One of the bylaws was that all officers had to own at least one emu or ostrich, so I bought Helen, a seven-year-old hen from Jesse. Helen laid 27 eggs the previous year, so it looked like a moneymaker. For me, she laid six eggs and stopped. The next year she laid none. That got me in trouble with my new bride, Margie, and it served me right.

Being an officer in the Co-op included all sorts of little duties that needed to be cleared immediately. We processed about 800 pounds of ostrich roasts and loins (the expensive cuts) and we needed a place to hold the meat temporarily in a freezer. I had room in my freezer that was stored in my mother-in-law's garage. The ostrich meat just fit into the freezer alongside some seafood that Billy sent me from Alaska.

This was August in Phoenix and it was hot, really hot. My mother-in-law had early Alzheimer's disease and she certainly didn't remember that we had the freezer filled with meat. In fact, she had no idea there was a freezer in her garage, so she pulled the plug to save electricity.

It took two days to lose the cool before the contents in the freezer spoiled. Two more days later, Mom called to say, "There are policemen at the house with a search warrant."

Margie was at her mom's house shortly before I got there and was sitting with her mom in her air-conditioned flower delivery van. The neighborhood stink bomb was a suspected dead body to the police. My mother-in-law smelled nothing.

I unlocked the garage and two policemen rushed past me to investigate inside and immediately backed out and vomited. I was trying to explain that it was a freezer malfunction, but they heard nothing apparently, so I was thinking, "Serves them right!"

The police disappeared about the same time Margie left to bring her mom to our house. That was about one minute after I opened the garage door!

That was the day I found out just how tough my new bride, Margie was, She helped me load the spoiled stuff and haul it to the landfill. The next chore took us into the wee hours to clean up the mess. The task was beyond the capability of my standby secret weapon to combat "stink".

Crest toothpaste helped but Stink won the battle. We scrubbed the freezer daily to deodorize it but in the end we "sold" the nearly new 20 cubic-foot appliance for $50. The garage smelled like rotten meat for the next five years.

The ostrich fad ran out of steam in Arizona by 2000. Many of the growers depended on the prices staying high for breeding stock, so they tucked away the experience as a lesson learned, somewhat satisfied to have earned a capital loss for their income tax returns.

Probably half the owners kept a few adult birds to raise food for the family. One hen laid so many eggs that the kids got tired of omelets. One ostrich egg was the equivalent of eighteen large chicken eggs.

Jesse and several growers survived, supplying high-end restaurants pricey cuts. Good hides still sold for at least four hundred dollars for a 14 square-foot tanned piece. The firemen stopped selling ostrich tenderloin sandwiches from their food trucks.

I believe the ostrich will emerge as a sustainable food source some day. The cost to feed a steer for two years, including the cost of its mother cow equaled the cost to feed fourteen ostriches for one year plus maintenance. The value of the 700 pounds of beef and the hide compared to 1750 pounds of high-priced ostrich meat plus hides worth four hundred dollars apiece had the ostrich profit advantage over beef by six to one.

There is a message in this story. Selling products in the Western economy isn't easy. In the case of having a sustainable market for ostrich meat, feathers, or hides there is a resistance to killing "Big Bird" or any kind of animal or bird with big cute eyes.

The people in China had no idea who "Big Bird" was. If it could be eaten, that was what mattered. All the time that we were wondering why all those fertile ostrich eggs were still selling for five hundred dollars each, it was the Chinese who supported that market. The eggs were shipped in state of the art incubators aboard ships, and they hatched shortly after reaching their new home.

The Chinese didn't eat those fertile eggs. Ostrich meat became popular, even though it was expensive. It was all consumed in China, so there was no exported ostrich meat. The ostrich leather exported from China that showed up in fashion products was another story. The biggest market for their leather handbags, shoes and coats is of course, the USA.

SHOCKWAVE

The 1996 Summer Olympics in Atlanta featured some memorable events, including a bombing, Muhammed Ali lighting the Olympic Torch, and a worldwide gathering of people espousing worldwide socialism. The event that thrilled me though was the TV story covering the European horses unloaded from airplanes and an explanation of the equipment unloaded right behind the horses.

The "star" was a large box on wheels containing what was called an Equitron, a shockwave machine designed to treat the equine athletes having arthritic problems with their tendons, ligaments and bones.

It was a wake-up call to vets like me who were practicing in the "stone age" of strong smelling liniments, recommended long rest times, secret remedy poultices and "firing", a painful treatment with hot needles or irritants. It was time we looked for a better way to treat sore horses.

Dr. Kent Allen was interviewed on the shockwave therapy and how it was applied to the horses participating in the Olympic equestrian events for the next ten days of the summer Olympics.

I was fascinated enough to research "shockwave" on my computer. There were articles about the physical characteristics of shockwaves as a type of energy and its use in lithotripsy to break up kidney stones in people. There was nothing in the search about lame horses. There were lots of references about pornography though.

It took me six more years before a new Versitron was delivered to my practice in Sun City West, Arizona. The new machine was a smaller, portable version of the large Equitron.

Since the horses featured in the old documentary were from France, Switzerland and Germany, I started searching again and looked up shockwave and lithotripsy in Europe. There it was in German! With the help of an English / German dictionary I found High Country Technologies, a Swiss company that had been manufacturing lithotripsy machines to treat for kidney stones in people for years. This time, there were many articles related to animals, along with many more sites about pornography.

The Equitron for horses and a smaller Versitron version were widely available for veterinarians all around the world.

My new computer was a lot smarter than I was. After a week of translating papers in German to English, my neighbor saw what was happening and politely pointed to the icon named "English" and said, "Push that button and watch what happens.

It was noted that in a German study using lithotripsy equipment as treatment for kidney stones in a group of elderly human patients, those with back problems all reported a big improvement in their arthritic backs. Further trials including different forms and locations of arthritis confirmed that shockwave force was indeed effective treatment for various skeletal problems.

The focus for early studies for people was as a treatment for planter fasciitis, often called "heel spurs".

A financial group approached me at this time with an interest in buying our veterinary practice in Sun City West. I was asked to remain as the clinic medical director and continued to work in the practice.

The new owners wanted to see if the shockwave addition as a new procedure would draw interest and be profitable.

It was too good an offer to be true. Margie was finishing her Masters degree in counseling and it was time to retire and cut back, since we were no longer "chasing cows".

Maybe it was too good to be true. When we received the down payment for the practice, it was handed over in a brown paper bag full of fifty-dollar bills that smelled like the back room of an old bar. There was enough money to buy a new Jeep, a computer and the shockwave machine with all the attachments and extra probes.

My venture with treating animals with extracorporeal shockwave treatment was just beginning. It was definitely not a toy and the learning curve was entirely up to me. The serial number on my unit was 000052 in the world so there was no cookbook to study. The general manager of the Swiss company wanted me to be a pioneer by trying the technique on all species of animals for all kinds of arthritis.

The first animal treated was on myself. I had sore feet from plantar fasciitis for several years so I sat down, put ultrasound gel on the bottom of my one foot and the physical therapist from the company applied 2000 shockwave pulses. I didn't know how to respond, so we did the same for the other foot.

The therapist told me that in a clinical trial, she had treated over four hundred people for heel spurs but never without pausing often because it was painful.

That day we had scheduled seven horses and three dogs for shockwave therapy. There was no time to waste waiting for the pain in my feet to subside. In fact, there was not that much pain, so we moved on. Six hours later my training was over, and so was the pain in my feet

That's when I realized what it was like being on the tip of a new technology. Some people like the excitement of being involved in a paradigm shift but most (veterinarians especially) are afraid to jump into an unproved technology. This was more than exciting! This technology allowed a veterinarian to address conditions that were untreatable at the time.

I learned a lot of information from other countries. More significantly, the results of my own patients, as the weeks passed were unbelievable. With time and trial, I learned a lot about the technology and how to best use the instrument.

The dog treated on the first day for bone spurs on her lumbar vertebrae (spondylosis) causing pain for the last three years showed improvement immediately. Within a month she was taken off her pain pills completely.

The two German Shepherd littermates with bad hips (hip dysplasia) treated on the first day improved to the point that neither showed any lameness in their movement three months later. They were also taken off their pain medication. What was spectacular was that all three of these dogs were over nine years old.

The horses didn't disappoint us. Not one horse showed any discomfort during shockwave therapy in spite of having no pain medication to numb the area treated. In fact, it became evident that horses have a spinal reflex response ("knee jerk response") when the exact sore spot was targeted with the shockwave "trode". The same reflex movement was noted on all species as I continued to learn about shockwave treatment. A knee jerk reaction had nothing to do with pain.

The standout treatment was on a Thorobred racehorse with a bone sequestration (bone chip) in his right shoulder. The X-rays showed a bone chip broken off the shoulder cuff the size of the end of my thumb, but thinner. The bone chip was completely torn away from the scapular bone, but still attached to all the ligaments and its blood supply. After two unsuccessful surgery attempts, this was his last chance. I swear that "Guy Fly" smiled at me while I gave a thousand pulses around that bone chip. Three weeks later, the X-rays confirmed that the bone density was gone, and so was his soreness.

Guy Fly never returned to the racetrack, but his luck was better than that. He was sold to a young lady who put him to work in showmanship equitation competition and for another twelve years he gave young riders a chance to learn how to ride a horse properly.

The day after having my feet treated I had a seminar in California for training in advanced laser surgery. There was also an introduction to shockwave therapy. My feet were feeling better after the shockwave treatment, but it wasn't until a spring shower forced me to run for cover that I realized how successful the treatment was. . The last time I ran was two years earlier. They were perfectly functional when running, and are still pain-free thirteen years later.

Selling pain tablets for arthritic dogs and horses was such a big part of being a veterinarian that I felt ashamed of myself. After using the shockwave treatment for spondylosis and leg lameness, our clinic revenue from sales of pain medicine dropped ninety percent. That meant a lot to me.

With the early shockwave treatment, most of the dogs were completely taken off their daily dose of pain meds within three weeks and needed only occasional pain relief for years. The shockwave treatments added comfortable years to their life spans.

I would like to state that every patient was cured forever, but that was far from the truth. Our results for approximately seven hundred dogs and two hundred fifty horses in the first five years were that eighty-five percent reacted dramatically and in some cases, immediately, showing complete function and vigor with all medication stopped at various times after their treatment.

Of the remaining fifteen percent, ten percent were unsuccessful either for being a high risk, and the rest were a "mystery why the dog did not respond. The last five percent were the "miracles" that were bad risks, but got better anyhow.

All things considered, shockwave therapy was a great treatment. Not perfect, but pretty darned good. No matter what species was treated, these percentages were consistent.

The workup on a canine with lameness was my favorite procedure, once all the equipment for diagnosing was in place in the clinic. Just plain common sense was the first tool to reach for. The rest of the tools, we had to purchase. A high definition digital X-ray machine, an in-house laboratory, and orthopedic surgery instruments were expensive, but necessary.

Our canine shockwave patients were brought to the clinic because they were in pain and could no longer play and perform their duty of making their humans happy with their presence.

Simply by observing the painful areas, by the way they moved, and in many cases by the way they couldn't move, most veterinarians had enough information to develop a base of data to build a diagnosis.

We developed a system for evaluating stages of lameness in dogs and used it to determine if shockwave treatment could deliver a high probability to improve their lameness. We were also able to deliver an accurate estimate of the cost of the treatment.

We evaluated the stages of lameness from Stage one; meaning the dogs were sore or traumatized and had no reason to use shockwave therapy, to Stage five; with dogs unable to get up without help and long-term arthritis. Euthanasia and end of life care had to be considered. Shockwave was considered counter-productive with those Stage five dogs and it was not recommended.

Horses fell into similar stages of lameness and responded with the identical percentages as we saw in dogs. That's where the similarity ended.

Injuries and overworked parts of the skeletal and ligament components caused about all the pain and lameness in the horses we treated.

Diagnosing the cause or even the location often was problematic. There were few instruments or machines that matched the experienced talents of the veterinarian and sometimes more so, the experience of the trainer or owner.

That statement leaves a lot of room for debate. Sometimes the horse owner thought he knew more than the vet and sometimes the owner believed he had the superior talent for diagnosis and treatment. I saw a lot of that, and sometimes those laymen did know more than I did.

Since I haven't spent my entire life working with horses, I usually listened very carefully to what the owner had to say. Ray Brown is an example.

Ray was a professional rodeo team roper. By all standards, he was one of the best. In fact, he is still a professional team roper after fourteen years, so there was no question about his talent. So what if he was a bit cocky? You have to be full of confidence in that business, and he was full of it.

He was heading into the National Finals Rodeo in Las Vegas, Nevada in a few months with "Sam", a strong Quarter Horse mare as his best roping horse in his string of six.

Sam was doing well, but there was something "off" with her. For some reason, Ray "knew" that Sam was "coming down with navicular". That's cowboy talk referring to an inflammatory and degenerating condition in a small bone between the last bone of the pastern and the toe bone.

The location and what it was connected to was responsible for the magic in the way horses placed their foot forward, then dig in to propel the thousand pound animal at speeds between thirty and forty miles an hour.

The deep digital flexor tendon is anchored in the space between the foot bones by an incredible matrix of tendon material and a bursa to complete a small joint. As the deep digital flexor tendon stretches and contracts it acts as a near version of perpetual motion. If anything went wrong with Sam's navicular area, she wasn't going to be a competitor in any calf roping for a long time.

I was one of only two veterinarians in Arizona with a shockwave machine at the time and several rodeo professional riders had good experiences with both of our services treating navicular disease. Rodeo folks were a close fraternity so the news traveled fast.

Ray's problem wasn't so much the horse being lame than it was in the last three months Sam bucked and threw Ray off on five occasions. Every time he got thrown, it happened in front of some pretty tough peers. A professional rodeo rider stayed on his horse, period! Ray did not like the heat he was getting from the other cowboys.

Ray had one thing right. If a trained horse bucks off a pro rider, there is something painful going on with the horse. Navicular was the popular lameness condition word of the time. When I drove up to the corral in central Arizona where Sam was in training, Ray greeted me with, "Doc, I want you to treat my horse for navicular."

Checking out Sam for lameness as she stood there showed nothing but a normal horse. Pressure applied to the foot and the navicular area had no reaction.

Next, we walked her out, trying to detect a flaw in her gait. I saw nothing that gave even anything that would lead me to figure out which front leg had a problem. "It's her left leg, you dummy", Ray shouted.

"I'm just starting", I replied, not completing the sentence that first came to mind. Becky, the trainer then rode Sam, and bingo, there it was! She was limping on her right front foot, and when she came around the arena in the opposite direction at a canter, the left front foot had a perceptible "hitch".

I had Becky dismount and hold Sam while I palpated the feet, legs, shoulder and back. Sam had a very sore back and that alone was a strong case for throwing a rider off. I knew that I had the perfect tool to treat Sam's back, and I also knew that my orders were to fix Sam's navicular disease.

My routine when treating a sore horse with shockwave therapy was to ask permission to scan all the possible locations capable of causing lameness and compensatory lameness. The probe of the shockwave machine was a great tool to find soreness. We set it at the lowest level of power and pressed the probe onto the skin covered with a layer of ultrasound gel. I went straight to the back and found a spot between the last three lumbar vertebrae that when the pulses were applied it practically brought the horse to her knees.

Ray yelled at me, "What in the hell are you doing, you quack? Go fix her foot, her left front foot!" Explaining something to this guy was going to be pretty touchy.

"I'm checking for at least one other sore spot. I replied. This back is sore enough to treat and if we find another soreness someplace I will treat that one too. If I fix Sam's navicular problem but don't take care of the sore back, you will still have a sore horse and my work would be worthless. Think of it as a tune up for Sam. Do you want me to continue or pack up and leave?"

"Go ahead and treat her," he grumbled. For a minute I thought he was going to beat up on me. I had quick thoughts of using the shockwave probe on him as a weapon if he tried.

The rest of the shockwave treatment was without any more disturbances from Ray. The neck on both sides was extremely sensitive, most likely damage from her early training days when she was tied short to a pole with a rope around her neck. This cruel practice used pain to teach the horse a lesson that trying to run away had strong painful consequences.

I noticed that Sam never turned her head when Becky rode her. The arthritis in her neck hurt if she turned her head to look around; Again, pain was the price for injuries inflicted years ago when Sam was a filly.

The left front foot did show enough pain to confirm inflammation in the lateral ligament in that front foot. The common condition was called "ring bone". If the horse had navicular syndrome, It would be detected with the shockwave machine. There would be a very noticeable response.

There was no reaction when he navicular area was scanned with the high setting, so there was no problem and no reason to waste pulses and money.

On a scale of pain from one to ten, the navicular area was a zero, the ringbone was a three, the neck on both sides was a nine and the back was an eight.

When we finished the treatment on Sam and cleaned the gel off, I spoke with Ray to explain what he needed to do to follow up on Sam regarding working her on a schedule where Ray would be competing off Sam within three weeks.

"Just give her three days rest for now, then ride her in a straight line. Be light on the halter for a week" I thought to myself, "If he ever gets thrown off again, it won't be Sam's fault."

For a second I thought Ray wasn't going to pay, but then he said, "Yeah, what do I owe you? Just be sure you write down the correct diagnosis on your receipt." He reached in his vest pocket and pulled out a roll of hundred dollar bills to pay me.

Ray and Sam did perform very well the next February at the National Finals Rodeo in team roping when they won the national championship. I was surprised when I read the article in a rodeo magazine about Ray Brown and his horse. The long article was about the comeback miracle of Ray's horse, Sam, with navicular disease and his treatment with the new fad, extracorporeal shockwave treatment. He even credited that vet in Arizona for saving his horse.

As I write this story it is fourteen years later. I retired for good and sold our practice in Prescott Valley, Arizona. The shockwave equipment went with the business and I miss it more than anything else associated with the practice. Maybe it's because I am eighty-one years old and my bones ache. My magic wand is out of my reach for the first time in fourteen years. I might have to do something about that.

The Day I Quit Treating Cows

September 12, 2001 (Just one day after the attack on the World Trade Center)

The mind works that way. Most of us remember in small details what we were doing when we absorbed the news on Nine Eleven, 2001. Dick, my brother-in-law recommended a book by a neurologist that turned out to be pretty interesting.

In the book, the author explains that the brain, as well as all the other organs and systems are "hard-wired" to save the life of the body it is entrusted to. It records and remembers "pictures" like a video whirring along at eighty frames a second, but in an emergency or eminent danger, the video slowed down to something like fifteen frames a second. The brain searches for danger very carefully to assess what parts of the body must react to and how to react.

Those carefully scrutinized "survival frames" are burned in the memory synapses and usually are played at will or when a trigger incident brings the traumatic episode back as a real incident. This has become known as post-traumatic stress disorder. My brain stored several of those episodes. Two experiences have a cow as the villain.

The incident with the cow that broke my neck on November 7th 1988 was remembered that way. The day that helped decide when it was time to quit chasing crazy cows and hang up my dusty cowboy boots was September 12, 2001. I can recall that episode in bright Technicolor, but it's a silent movie.

My dusty boots and plastic sleeves were ready to go to work that morning outside of Wickenburg. The task for the day filled me with satisfaction. This was working with cattle in the true West in the beautiful warm autumn desert on a perfect day.

Real cowboys gathered sixty desert Longhorn cows, confining them in a corral. My job was to sort out the pregnant cows from those that were not pregnant. That's where the plastic sleeves came in handy.

The corral was located ten miles east of Wickenburg, Arizona, in a wide valley along the Hassayampa River. This was the kind of vet call that was really enjoyable, ordinarily. We had no idea that we would be introduced to the devils own herd!

The corral in the desert was a very old drop-off station constructed with railroad ties secured by twisted barbed wire. My guess was that this corral hadn't changed for forty years and my assessment on its functional containment capability was that it barely squeezed into the "Just might work" category.

The cows, on the other hand were in good condition, big and strong. It took the genetics of the Longhorn breed to survive that hostile environment and that was what faced us that morning – cows with long horns!

The chute was sturdy and it took the same kind of man to operate the catch quickly enough to hold the cows before they squirmed through and back into the desert where they wouldn't be seen for two more years. After getting to know my cowboy helpers, it was clear there was only one sober worker and he was not one of the cowboys, so the stanchion at the end of the chute job fell to me.

The stanchion was designed to catch the cow between the head and the shoulder. As quickly as humanly possible, an old bent two-inch diameter pipe was thrust behind the cow in the chute so she couldn't back out. The long horns made this process a lot more difficult, along with an equal measure of danger.

The next course was to determine if the cow was pregnant or not and how far along she was in her pregnancy. I had been doing this for forty years and this was the first time there was a concern that we might run into trouble somehow.

After checking the cows one-by-one, the pregnant ones were turned back out into the desert with a large number on their right rump indicating how many months pregnant they were. The "open", or non-pregnant cows were directed into a holding pen to wait for a truck to haul them someplace else not so pleasant. Only three cows of the sixty did not make the pregnant list, and those three cows found their way out in the pasture by being smarter than we were.

One of the cowboys named "JP" got ran over by a runaway non-pregnant longhorn and the other two open cows followed her through the gate. At least, the non-pregnant cows were identified as such (no markings). The cowboys had a name for the pasture. They called it, "Way out yonder".

We were down to three cows that were studying us for a weakness in our work habits. They probably got dizzy with information overload.

Usually when we finished checking a cow for pregnancy and marked the rump, "Butsy", the other cowboy, was supposed to mark down the ear tag. That was the only job he was allowed to do, so I figured he couldn't do much harm, besides, he wasn't feeling well. He made a lot of trips to the water jugs in the cooler. That was good; at least he wouldn't get dehydrated.

Butsy was as skinny as a pencil. He also was not very good with a pencil. He started out all right, but instead of marking down a "B-67 Yellow" it soon regressed to doodling, especially nude women. His pencil had to be taken away from him. Butsy was classified as, "officially worthless".

"JP" was easily a hundred pounds overweight. He actually worked pretty hard because he did everything the hard way. He used his body to push sixty ornery cows one at a time into the chute. By the end of the day he was red faced, dripping with sweat and he too, made lots of trips to the cooler.

When working these shy desert cows, it's expected that one out of ten cows won't be so shy and will turn back and charge the people handling the gate of the chute. When that happened, the survival instincts kicked in and we turned to the corral fence and climbed over it. The goal was not to be there when the cow hit the fence.

Something went haywire in our finely tuned operation. A speckled momma cow went out thirty feet, looked back at us and charged. Butsy and I picked the same part of the corral to climb over. Our bodies collided and neither of us made it over.

It was a scary sight (especially in slow motion) to see an angry cow pointing her nose at the strange pile of clumsy men on the ground. Oh—oh! I'm looking up at the cow from under Butsy, so I must be part of that clump of the two stupid men on the ground. Thundering hooves (making no sound) turning up the sand, cockleburs and coming fast! (In slow motion). It was an awesome sight to see the sun shining off those polished black horns, easily spanning seven feet across, aimed at the pile of two men still wondering what happened.

In slow motion, the thought came through, "Wait a minute! How come the horns are so polished?" and your brain said, "It's because she knows how to use them, you dummy." Lying on the ground with Butsy on top of me there was no way to reach safety for either of us. I was thinking fast, but in slow motion, "That's good, maybe the cow with the big horns won't see me". Then the video in my brain stopped.

The cow's nose was less than a foot away. She shook those big black horns, then shook her head again and walked away. I knew what she was thinking; "Damn fools. Not worth messing up my curly hair between my beautiful shiny black horns." Thanks to the cow, we were embarrassed, but alive.

We all had enough, including the cows, and especially my cowboy helpers. Butsy left the last cow out to join the herd. We went over to gather our gear and head out for Wickenburg to drop these guys off at the McDonalds where they were picked up earlier in the day.

I took a long drink of water and noticed there were three one-gallon jugs of water when we started. I was looking at two full jugs and one was empty. That was the one I just emptied. In a gully behind a scrub chaparral bush were two-dozen empty cans of Coors Light! That got my respect for the resiliency of the American Cowboy.

Why would anybody drink cold water on a hot day when there was perfectly good beer? Well, maybe it wasn't good beer anymore; when the cowboys hid the case of beer in the morning shade it was cool, but as the day progressed it probably didn't matter to them anymore.

They were drunk and I never noticed. I thought they were out of shape and I was working them too hard.

When Margie de-briefed me for the details of my call out Wickenburg way, her comment was, "Doc, you shouldn't be doing work like that anymore. You are sixty-seven years old. For gosh sakes think about working with small animals full time." Hate to say it but you're right." I answered. So this was the day I quit treating cows.

ENDSLOW

Endslow is a little brown dog, a legend in his own mind and mine as well. He believed God made him love all humanity, friendly dogs, and treats. The devil decreed that he must hate and kill gophers, skunks, rats, and rattlesnakes.

He simply had to be a part of every function in the lives of his people family, which included every person on earth. You will see his presence in almost all of the pictures we take. If you look closely at the cover picture of this book, you will see a little brown tail wagging at the bottom of the lovely pasture scene. Margie took a picture of Delaney and me just seconds after Endslow killed a chipmunk. He was so happy to show us his prize.

Endslow was terribly abused in his other life. That life was before Margie brought him to our house in Paulden. He belonged to Jeremy; a client Margie was counseling in her practice specializing in juvenile offenders.

Jeremy showed up for his appointment cradling this little brown dog in his arms. Both Jeremy and Endslow were crying, Endslow in pain and Jeremy in another kind of pain.

"What's the story?" Margie asked. Jeremy came from a severely broken home situation and was currently living with an uncle who treated the dog badly. This time his uncle repeatedly kicked the dog like he was a football, resulting in broken bones. The poor dog had no function of his right hind leg.

"I have to find him a good home. My uncle keeps kicking him, and he is going to kill him some day."

Margie told him, "I will find him a home. I'll take him home, and Doc will fix him, but there is no way he is going back to your uncle."

"What's your dog's name? Margie asked. "Well, I call him Endslow," Jeremy answered. "Why?" Margie asked. "Because his end is low," Jeremy explained

Margie told him not to worry, she would take Endslow, but he won't be coming back, Margie said. "We'll fix him up, and you can visit him anytime. I'll even have him here for your sessions so you can hold him and see how he's doing. Then I will find him a loving home."

On examining Endslow, his legs were not broken, but his pelvis was. And his urine had blood in it, so off we went to the Sun City West clinic we sold but still worked there three to four days a week.

Radiographs confirmed the leg bones were intact, but the pelvis had at least twenty bone shards going in all directions. The bladder was OK, just a few broken vessels and the kidneys looked normal.

Surgery on Endslow was beyond my capability and would be a challenge for a specialist. My orthopedic surgeon colleagues advised against surgery and discussed what was going on with the skeletal muscles and ligaments about the pieces of bones floating around. Endslow was able to walk — just not well.

With positive experience using our shockwave equipment in similar cases, we decided that rest wouldn't be enough. Our decision was to use my shockwave equipment to stimulate the healing process.

With time, the ligaments attached to muscle bundles on one end and bone on the other end were expected to bring the bone fragments close to where they belonged anatomically.

Extracorporeal shockwave therapy was projected to stimulate rapid bone attachment as well as dissolving bone fragments having no source of blood supply.

By the time I applied shockwave therapy, a week had passed since the kicking incident. A lot of migration of the various pieces of bone was already in the process of closing into something more normal. We felt the crunching of his pelvis when Endslow tried to move. With the help of a mild sedative and moving slowly, Endslow endured a half hour of shockwave pulses (2,000 in all) without one peep of disagreement.

The response was phenomenal! He stood on his right hind leg, which he had not been able to use since he was kicked. Three weeks later he was walking around on all four legs. Exercise outdoors hastened his recovery to near normal movement, although his right side is noticeably lower, so he is a walking advertisement for his name, "End's Low." No further treatments were necessary, and he has returned to his natural 90%; unless he gets excited, then he was the fastest dog in any pack!

Our house in Paulden was on the fringe of civilization. We watched antelopes give birth to their babies from our back porch. Rattlesnakes sunned themselves on our east patio in the mornings, and Coyotes were an everyday sighting. They called to our dogs to play, sounding like dogs, not coyotes.

One day Endslow answered and slipped through the front door to play with three coyotes. He was gone and had other notions rather than coming back when called. Following Endslow and his three playmates was impossible. They disappeared into the gorge behind the house, running and nipping each other with Endslow doing most of the nipping. We tried to brace ourselves, thinking the worst, but fifteen minutes later all four of them were heading to the house.

At about a hundred yards from the house, the coyotes broke away and headed back into the gorge. Endslow was covered with coyote slobber, very thrilled to have such wonderful playmates.

For several years Endslow was Margie's constant assistant at the counseling office, curling up on the top of the couch as close to the patient's neck as possible unless there was a need for him to perform his therapy; allowing the kids to pet and cuddle him.

Margie's partner Sydnee begged to have Endslow with her clients too, so he was a busy and a happy associate. Sydnee called him the C.E.O (Chief Excrement Officer) because of the presents he left in the office from time to time.

Today, Endslow is like me: growing old "grayfully", taking naps and enjoying his retirement. He really likes fishing because there are chipmunks to chase.

RABIES

By Emmy White, after her Grandpa told her a forty-eight year old story about a "mad dog".

My Grandpa tells me the story of the dog with rabies that messed up his day. Just so you know, this happened so long ago my mom wasn't even born yet, and there were no cell phones, or television, or even air-conditioning. They did have cars that went very fast on gravel roads. That's weird.

My Grandpa just finished helping a cow, and somehow made it better, and he was driving back into town. Then the town constable blocked the road in front of Grandpa yelling, "Stop! There's a dog down by the river that's got "rabbies." That is rabies, a deadly disease that can be spread to people. The cop spoke kinda funny I guess.

The constable led the way to where the dog was. The dog's mouth was open and his tongue was way out and foamy saliva was dripping all over. His eyes were rolled way back like they were looking at the inside of his head. He looked dumb and scary at the same time.

The constable, Barney Bumblehauf was standing behind my Grandpa and asked, "That dog got rabbies?" When Grandpa said, "It sure looks like rabies", the constable pulled out his gun and shot the dog in the head.

Grandpa couldn't hear anything but a loud bell ringing in his head because Barney blasted the gun off next to his right ear. The dog's blood and brains went everywhere and some got on Grandpa's face, including in his eyes.

Grandpa told me that rabies is caused by a virus and is very dangerous especially when the virus in saliva, the brain, and blood gets splattered into the eyes. The virus spread quickly to nerves and then travels somehow to the brain. When it gets into the nerves in the eye, it is awfully close to the brain, so it doesn't take long to kill a person. If the virus reached the brain, it always resulted in a horrible death.

But Grandpa didn't die, so I know that did not happen. What did happen was Grandpa got mad and took Barney's gun and threw it into the river and probably cussed a little because he does that sometimes. Then he put the dead dog in a bag and drove two hours at eighty miles an hour to the state laboratory.

The laboratory people did a special stain of the brain tissue and looked at it under a microscope and said that it was positive for rabies. The state health big shot who was alerted that a serious case of rabies exposure was coming was there to give Grandpa his first shot in the belly. My Grandpa says that it felt like a baseball bat to the stomach. He needed a shot in the belly every day for two weeks.

He said that after five days he was scared he would die. After five more days he was afraid he wouldn't die. Grandpa took all 14 shots and didn't die, but he was sick and sore for two more weeks and he lost a lot of weight.

As for Barney, he wasn't allowed to have a gun anymore. Barney didn't lose his job, probably because nobody wanted it. He wasn't paid very much. Grandpa thinks it wasn't much more than $50 a month, so Barney stayed on for years, protecting Fort Recovery as best he could, which I think is weird.

Let's do it Again

After forty-four years in veterinary service Margie and I decided we were at a good point in our life to consider retirement, but with some caveats. I retained ownership of the shockwave equipment but still performed therapy for the new owner of our Sun City Wes practice.

We were also scheduling shockwave treatment for horses and dogs at different vet clinics and at the clients close to our new home.

That with my garden, fishing trips, and politics, I succeeded in staying out of Margie's domain in the kitchen. Our new neighborhood was in Pauldin, Arizona and it gave us all we wished for; especially having the grandchildren living nearby.

There was enough spare time to get involved in water conservation and make a difference forming local political sustainable measures to make sure there would be enough water for future generations in our part of the state.

I was semi-retired and loving it. Margie was working full time as a counselor, specializing in juvenile offenders during the day and traveling long distances two nights a week for classes leading to her first Masters degree.

Looking back, that seems very busy, but that pace for each of us suited us well; especially since our grandchildren were just down the road.

Four years of this idyllic life later we opened our new animal hospital. So much for semi-retiring; the fruit of three years of planning and construction were now ready for us to go back to work. The new clinic was the remedy for that feeling there was something missing.

This chapter is the short version of the next eight years that ended up defining who we were and what we were capable of accomplishing, once challenged.

I never appreciated the effect of two people united in purpose and talent. Working side by side from the beginning of a goal to the finish, until we as husband and wife decided to work together on this big project. The possibilities were tremendous. The best outcome would be to call it a love story.

We picked a spot to build our animal hospital that demographically had it all; a major highway went past our property and had a finished construction date by the time our veterinary clinic would be built. The north side of Prescott Valley where we decided to build had scant veterinary service, and a sizeable population flanked the location where every household had on average two dogs. Many nearby prospective clients had horses and farm animals.

The location was also 28 miles from where we just built a new home. It made sense to consider moving from Paulden to the Prescott Valley vicinity because the drive was already more than an hour to reach Prescott Valley. Highway 89, the main conduit between Prescott and Chino Valley was in the progress to be upgraded from a narrow dangerous two-lane road to a four-lane freeway with a median. The bad news was that the road was projected to be five years before construction would be completed.

There were two more reasons to leave our beautiful home on the Verde Gorge. Our daughter's family moved to Payson, taking our grandchildren with her, so now they will be 130 miles farther away. Being closer to the grandchildren played big in the decision to retire and make our first move.

The second event was completely unexpected. A local real estate agent rang the doorbell one Saturday afternoon to tell us he had a buyer who wanted our house and didn't care how much it cost. All of a sudden, those darned stars lined up for us again. In less than 24 hours, the house was sold!

The clinic building process took three years before we opened the doors for our first client. Every client after the first had to be earned. There were no client lists to buy and there was no existing practice to take over.

This was the million-dollar practice we were wishing for; we owed over a million dollars by the time we stocked the supplies, bought equipment, and hired a staff of five.

We weren't just building a vet clinic. We also bought an eight-acre lot in a pretty green valley with a running creek all summer.

For a year we lived in a fifth-wheel trailer with two dogs two cats and often accommodated our son and son-in-law who were building our new home for us. The time flew by and the running creek ran dry. We were so busy, but we were also very happy that we decided to do this.

Margie knew more about construction than I did by far. For me, it was the best experience in the world to design and build a veterinary hospital. Of course there were all kinds of engineers to advise us but the design of how to plan every concept to direct the clinic property into a working structure packed with new ideas was my baby.

The aim was to construct a building that would be perfectly functional for generations, efficient to heat and cool, one that would be easily kept sanitary, and would not smell bad (a problem for too many animal facilities). In the end it had to be beautiful, and it was!

Amid the hustle and bustle of construction, I decided to get involved in politics. I had enough spare time to get involved in water conservation and make a difference by helping local officials develop sustainable measures to assure there would be water for future generations.

After the house was built, I ran for a seat on the Dewey-Humboldt Town Council and won my election. By the end of my four-year term as a council member, we were very busy in the new veterinary clinic. The Town Council demanded all the physical and mental time I had. What a great experience though! Our twice-monthly meetings debated and decided issues important to the growth and management of the town without pay.

It became clear that Margie and I would have to work side by side through the process of managing everything dealing with the practice, even before we opened. Once in operation, Margie managed all the things except the professional clinical practice. I devoted myself to strictly do the things the doctor is expected to do. Managing was not my strong suit, but it was Margie's strength.

One day Margie asked if I thought she was a good practice manager. That's like your wife asking, "Does this make me look fat?" She was still learning the skills rapidly and was attending practice management seminars every chance that came up. She was on track to be the best practice manager in the county. A year later I could answer that question easily, telling her she was the best ever, anywhere.

By that time, Margie closed out her counseling practice to work full time (and no pay) for the clinic.

The very first dog we saw in the new clinic was Blackie, an old black lab with an aggressive cancer of those darned anal glands. The cancer metastasized to the lungs. The big beautiful black dog with soft pleading in his eyes was going to die because no veterinarian ever checked the size and density of his anal glands.

"That's what the groomer is supposed to do" was the answer Blackie's previous vet gave me when I asked about Blackie's history. If the growth was found early, a simple surgery with a laser removed the gland with the tumor inside the sac. Dogs don't need the things anyhow and this procedure saved the lives of many dogs.

As our practice grew rapidly, we did find a lot of dogs with this cancer. Surgery was curative, so this was one of the most satisfactory surgeries that we offered. We were in the business of saving lives of animals and it all started with a rectal examination.

The first year's income from July 2007 to a year later, was surprisingly above our expectations, but we had more expenses than we had income, which was expected, thanks to 27% of the annual income going for payment of debt on the building.

The second year was 2008, the year that a quarter of our clients were out of work. We were hit full force by the recession of 2008. Our prices were frozen for the next four years. The only answer we had was to work harder, smarter, and longer to provide the highest level of service.

We increased production by 40% for each of the next two years. That did not mean we made a big profit, but it was a good indication that some day we would. All that time, we were paying high percentage loan interest plus late fees way too often.

As any service organization that expects to grow knows it must nurture what it takes to grow: service, and that means more better trained people who are worth more salary. That also included an associate veterinarian full-time.

Between the fifth and sixth year was the hardest on us as owners. We cashed in all our savings, and refinanced the house for cash to meet paydays. An unexpected stock closeout Margie had for twenty years saved us again. Selling the tractor was the last straw. We ran out of assets to draw from.

Finally in the sixth year we were able to get our head above the water, financially. If we wanted to position the practice as a good opportunity for a new veterinarian owner, we had to show that we could sustain that pattern of profitability for three years in a row.

Our time line to be ready to sell the practice was extended two extra years. We were in position to sell the practice in eight years instead of the five or six years as we first planned.

Our goals when we started planning were to build a clinic for half of what it really cost, build a clientele by practicing good medicine and a caring attitude, then grow to a million dollar production goal, and sell to an enthusiastic veterinarian. We expected to help in the transition to full ownership.

My clock was an unknown, that is: How long could "Doc" effectively work in the practice? We were well past the fifty years party and the ten-minute naps were more frequent on my Laz-Y-Boy Chair.

We achieved all of our goals three years late. We wouldn't change anything in how it worked out. Money was part of our goal of course, but the last practice was by far the best. We practiced excellent care with good equipment and skill. Every person working in the practice had the opportunity to grow into proficiencies that made them more valuable and their pay increased with their worth.

So, to answer the question, "Was it worth the scary times financially, the energy it took to get the patients' notes finished every day, and in the end, leaving your chosen vocation?"

For Margie and myself, this was the best of everything. Our clients were our friends. We knew their family members by name, including their pets. Our work was beyond just care; it was love, confidence and a high level of skill. I would gladly volunteer for another fifty-three years. Unfortunately, my body was pre-planned to wear out.

Prescott Valley was a good town, and we felt that the community gave us so much support the whole time.

Margie made everything fall into place, whether it wanted to or not.

That woman inspired awe in me and I love her dearly. The teamwork never let down.

After we left the practice, our lives still raced along, but without the anxiety of facing another payroll. Certainly we missed the hustle and energy of a busy day at the clinic, but these days when we wake up at eight O'clock in a quiet house we look around and say to ourselves, "This is nice."

Fly Catcher
Author Photograph

FLY CATCHER

I saved this story for the last chapter, not because anything stopped, but because it was a transition event that spanned my experiences as a practicing veterinarian and the years after retirement.

My professional life, you may have noticed, seemed punctuated with spurts of passion for new ideas, new places to discover, and above all, new experiences with people and their animals.

The Sarracenia (pitcher plant), or what they call it in the bayous of Mississippi, the "Fly Catcher", entered my life five years ago, at a time I was not in search for another passion. Maybe this remarkable plant was looking for me. No, I didn't discover it. I am sure it was discovered many times during its existence for the past twenty million years.

Everything in my life seemed to start with a casual remark. I don't recall asking, "What's going on in your life that makes you excited?" The stories just came spontaneously. Sometimes I felt like a lightening rod.

Harry, a retired financial advisor and current gold trader told the story about his long time neighbor introducing him to a natural medicine made from the Sarracenia purpura plant.

I received a small jar of the stuff with the vague advice to use it on anything that goes bad regarding the skin. Within a month, I was conducting case studies on animals in my practice at the request of a group of scientists from the state university who were conducting their own research on cancer case studies in people with this same product.

It did not take very long before I was satisfied what this natural product did for any skin lesions. It cured yeast infections, burns, and it quickly healed severe lacerations, closing quickly, leaving no scars.

The extract from the plant's "stomach" was a powerful pain reliever, anti-viral, and to a surprising degree, it is in laboratories being studied as an anti-cancer treatment. Insect, spider, and rattlesnake bites were resolved in days, sometimes in minutes. It also works on lips to kill the Herpes simplex virus and heal the common cold sore.

The more it proved its effectiveness in many applications, the more I was afraid of its demise, like extinction.

If this natural medicine replaced just a few brands like "Band-Aid" or "Abreva", the supply of Sarracenia plant that would be needed to make a natural product the American source for this plant would be extinct in a year.

Another problem was that something this simple, yet effective, wouldn't be able to compete with existing established brands that gave our country the best medical service in the world. It would take millions of dollars to market the product to compete in the established market

All this plant needed to survive were three simple things: a swamp with leached out soil, a quadrillion mosquitoes, and to be left alone

Native Americans used this plant as folk medicine one hundred fifty years before we got so excited about its benefits. Those Native American descendants and advisors felt it was not the time to introduce this treasure at this time and in this country. As folk medicine, it was important to them. They say, "First, find a way to bring back Sarracenia like it was a hundred years ago in America, or grow it in another country".

My focus with this project was to keep my family and friends supplied with our 'folk medicine" and to possibly develop a foundation to save this remarkable plant growing in the "American Amazon", the Mobile-Tenshaw Delta in the Gulf states.

It is time to declare some of these plants at least "Endangered Species", and work on sustainable growing practices.

First, let's talk about this strange, beautiful and remarkable plant. Sarracenia is a diversified species that in all cases are carnivorous, that is, the plant received all its nourishment except water from insects and small animals, birds and even pollen from the air.

As the plant received nutrients it did more than sustain growth, reproduction, and nutrient storage in the roots, as other plants do. In addition, this plant maintained a nascent (born to and added to linked data: Webster Dictionary) immune system that has been going on for an estimated 20 million years that was part of its DNA.

The Sarracenia plant's immunity was carried throughout generation after generation within its' reproduction cells, down to the DNA strands replicating the last generation of information to the next. More recently, as with each growing season the glands imbedded in the inside of the "pitcher" were exposed to hundreds of organisms, toxins, spores, bacteria, viruses, and on and on. Our immune system responded to those things also and our bodies developed immunity the same way.

In this plant, for instance, if a mosquito carried one of the viruses that cause dengue fever fell prey to the plant and was digested by the plant's juices, that virus was digested as well.

The dengue fever virus DNA carried by the mosquito would most likely be recognized by the plant's immune system. Then an increased antiviral immune response to the dengue virus would be made and the product of that response resided in the tissue of the plant.

The wonder of Nature is in the magnitude of all the molecules, even atoms that stimulate an immune response within that plant throughout its growing cycle. Add to that, the 20 million growing cycles having a presence in the genetic reproductive cells make this plant a grand repository of immune responses.

Maybe that thought is true; but maybe it isn't. It would be extremely difficult to determine. I believe in the camp that supports generation of DNA linking current data to ancestral data until science convinces me otherwise.

This plant has the ability to carry immunity against viruses, yeast, and organisms that inhabit other parts of the world; not necessarily from the swamps of America. That's something to think about.

What do we have here? The answer is, we have a plant that is treated to extract these immunity and antitoxin particles as a medicine. We have a "Folk Medicine" like so many other natural extracts.

The perfect folk medicine is one that has been in use for centuries, even better, thousands of years that performs consistently in a positive manner with no bad effects. A few adverse reactions may be tolerated if it did not cause death, but would aid in the relief or cure of a scourge like smallpox.

Smallpox is exactly an example of such a scourge that was cured with the Sarracenia purpura tea made from its roots in the Canadian plains 150 years ago (Morris, Lancet 1862).

The published story appeared in the British medical journal describing the experience of a Canadian Army medical doctor during an outbreak of smallpox involving military personnel and the local Mic-Mac Indian community. An old Mic-Mac woman, "Old Sally Paul" made a tea from the roots of the pitcher plants identified as Sarracenia purpura. This tea when given to patients in the final hours of their expected death cured every person who drank the tea. Those who refused the strong tasting medicine all died.

So where are now? A big step backward from 1862, I believe. Wetlands, the places where this plant grows have dwindled down to five percent since 1862. The Sarracenia plants number only two percent of those growing in Civil War days. Without meaningful intervention, we will see the extinction of this plant in our lifetime

What can we do? Work for sustainability of the Sarracenia species in the areas where the plant grows. This may be the easiest part since this plant is designed by Nature to survive. It is possible to bring the plant numbers back to what they were one hundred fifty years ago. That would be the first step.

Regarding making the natural medicine, we need field trials on animals in big numbers, followed by human trials, not conducted and paid for by the pharmaceutical industry, but by doctors and academia, funded by ground-swell donations from the population as in the research funded for cancer cure.

Having the natural medicine, or folk medicine in the marketplace would follow as the last step.

"Folk medicine" is not scientifically based. It is the result of trial and errors over a long history. If the treatment works well, consistently, and without dangerous side effects and is affordable, then the use of that medicine will be the drug of choice over time. The reason is simply that "It works".

Why have underdeveloped countries that depend on folk medicine as their first choice (or only choice) not picked up on the Sarracenia species as a source of natural therapy? The most likely answer is that the plant does not grow in their part of the world. Sarracenia grows only in a very specific ecosystem, suitable for specific varieties for that ecosystem. Those countries having favorable growing conditions would be a good place to have the medicine accepted, providing the cost is affordable.

If this were a cottage industry with certified extracted material consistently of high quality available at free market prices, the cost for the finished product has a chance of being universally affordable.

You can't blame "Big Pharm" for the high price of their products. The price for research and development is hard to imagine. New products have a very high mortality in the process of research and development. Developed civilizations and their drug manufacturers buy into "The Molecule" search for new drugs, and our drug enforcement agency (DEA) cannot protect its citizens from dangers found in natural medicine products with hundreds of "molecules" in a single product. I think we are looking at the answer and simply don't recognize it

Education and communication holds the key somehow. Both allotropic and natural medicines have their values and dangers, and we have the DEA to guide the process with safety as their single goal. My guess is that there are a rather small number of safe and effective "folk medicine" offerings that can be sustainably harvested, and for allotropic medicine, there will always be discoveries to meet health challenges coming from pure science.

In the meantime, the "cottage industry" model makes sense in less advanced countries from the start, but it would be looked at within the domain of the large pharmaceutical companies in developed countries as competition. It shouldn't be that way.

Sometimes, smaller is more efficient. For instance, a family unit can process two tons of biomass or more in a year, employing benchtop equipment at a low capital investment and send out more than half a million tubes ready for the market. In that process, each small business supports five to ten small family farm units quite handsomely, and is rewarded with a good profit for their entrepreneurial efforts.

Now, after abusing the power of the "Bully Pulpit" of the writers' desk, I apologize. I cannot apologize for having passion.

My life has been blessed by opportunities, ideas to explore, and the passion that fuels the oxygen to do something about those opportunities. I only wish that I were as smart as I thought I was. I will settle with three out of four. With good health, passion and luck, this may lead to something really good.

ABOUT THE AUTHOR

"Doc"
Author Photograph

Dr, Tebbe is a veterinarian who actively practiced for fifty-three years, beginning in his Midwestern hometown as a farm animal vet. Technology and paradigm shift movements lured his him to the Western states of Arizona and California.

His passions for community involvement, his profession, and public health were strongly prompted by a life-long love of animals and wonders of nature. The best moment in his vocation was the growth of recognition for the animal-people bond.

This is his first publication as a book.